T0146954

BOLDLY TRAVEL
HERO

BOLDLY TRAVEL
HERO

PETER COHEN

BOLDLY TRAVEL HERO

iUniverse books may be ordered through booksellers or by contacting:

iUniverse
1663 Liberty Drive
Bloomington, IN 47403
www.iuniverse.com
1-800-Authors (1-800-288-4677)

Because of the dynamic nature of the Internet, any web addresses or links contained in this book may have changed since publication and may no longer be valid. The views expressed in this work are solely those of the author and do not necessarily reflect the views of the publisher, and the publisher hereby disclaims any responsibility for them.

Any people depicted in stock imagery provided by Getty Images are models, and such images are being used for illustrative purposes only.
Certain stock imagery © Getty Images.

ISBN: 978-1-5320-5832-5 (sc)
ISBN: 978-1-5320-5833-2 (e)

Print information available on the last page.

iUniverse rev. date: 09/18/2018

1. B – brain, sleepcare

2. O – oral supplementation

3. L – less food

4. D – diet

5. *L – less toxins*

6. Y – youth

7. T – new technologies

8. R – relax

9. A – anticancer

10. V – blood vessels

11. E – exercise

12. L – logotherapy and mental health

13. H – heart and spirit

14. E – eros

15. R – recovery

16. O – optimal conditions

Many types of fitness

1. emotional

2. physical

3. spiritual

4. social

5. intellectual

6. financial

BOLDLY TRAVEL HERO

An unprecendented book on human development that is multi-faceted and greatly in need.

Spiritual Fitness

Spiritual fitness is a matter of having a good relationship with a deity, as one understands him and a good relationship with yourself. It comes from one's conscience, which is the essence of both courage and maturity. Someone who is mature, takes responsibility for what he does, and feels guilty if he does something wrong. He can then face the consequences of what he has done. An example of this was a man who turned himself in to the police after thinking he committed a crime because he felt guilty and faced the consequences. This was a courageous thing to do. The righteous gentiles who sheltered Jews from the Nazis acted out of conscience and courage. In an opposite example, some teachers and principals sent me to an abusive school, like people who turned us in to the Nazis, to face certain failure and death at these people's hands. They deluded themselves into thinking they did something right, and that death and suffering was good for us. These were despicable people.

Overcoming Fear and Being A Hero or How Science Can Increase Courage

In order to have courage, you must want to do something and decrease the fear which might prevent you from doing it. Courage and/or lack of it is not a matter of genetic inferiority or inferiority, as my family would like to believe I am genetically inferior. If you want to do something, you can probably do it. Fear is decreased by exercise, practice, and relaxation. If one does not want to do something, it is OK not to do it and he or she should not berate him or herself for not doing it. Our survival instincts require that we must respect fear and pain. Also, courage without potentially helping someone is not really a virtue and has not moral value. Il faut (d'abord) durer is a good credo summed up in

"The time comes when a writer better be in good shape, with good legs and a power punch, ready to fight like hell until the bitter dying end." - to improve the well-being of others I must add.

Any decrease of anxiety must use two principles. (1) You must learn to handle the situation using progressive overload, doing no more than you are relatively comfortable doing. Also (2) you must rid the fear in the fear situation or visualization of the fear situation. Visualization and actual practice both work.

Also, training, which gives you confidence and a feeling of well-being, such as strength and endurance or a specific skill such as skydiving or self-defense, or boxing helps. Listing what you want to do and steps to achieving it helps.

I should also mention that I have known fear, pain, illness, and looked at death, as anyone has. Sometimes I have handled it well and othertimes not. Someone who is immune to fear, pain or suffering is either abnormal or dishonest. The biggest myth of courage is that it is inborn, either you have it or you don't. My family thinks that I have no courage and am genetically inferior. They mockingly call me a GI. My action speak for themselves. There is no such thing as genetically inferior or superior. Courage depends on wanting to have it. If you do not want it, it is not a problem because you just will not get what you do not want, which is good.

Will power is to courage as iron is to steel. Will power hones and improves courage so that when you improve your will power muscle you improve your courage potential. Again, it is not genetic and is a matter of wanting to do it. It is honed by daily discipline, knowledge and skill, practice, feeling good, and believing that you can do it. Whether you think you can or think you can't, either way you are right.

Also, stay away from harming yourself or others. Even heroic actions are uncalled for. We are here to help help others and primum non nocere (first to do no harm). Wanting to help others, loving attitudes, and a sense of responsibility, embodied in conscience, is helpful. Also, iron performs the same function as steel so that will power is courage is courage tweaked by a pride or dignity in one's behaviour. Pride or dignity is perhaps the most important factor. Risking life, limb and enduring pain is not useful. Guns, war, and military service is not useful. However, any disciplinary training is useful as military training increases courage. Quaker disciplines are helpful. Getting out of your comfort zone is helpful as long as it is not too far out.

When someone is able to do something or not do something, there is always a reason for it. Even though my family thinks I am not courageous, and immature and irresponsible due to genetics, this is not only not true, but again there is no such thing as genetically superior or inferior.

Overcoming Fear

Overcoming fear has been a lifelong experience for me. Relaxation and systemic desensitization are helpful. I will describe them in this work.

Systematic desensitization consists of finding ten to twelve situations of an area that you fear. For example, open spaces.

1. a small open space

2. empty halls

3. crowded halls

4. a large open space

5. a vast, wide, continuous open space

6. a massive, perspective as in skydiving

7. riding a horse or running through wide open spaces

8. walking close to the middle of a wide open space

9. walking along the side of a wide open space

10. walking along the middle of a small open space

11. crowded parking lots

12. empty parking lots

We number these in the order we have difficulty, use relaxation that I will describe elsewhere in this work, and go into the situations until you master them without fear. Then proceed to the next most difficult situation.

For assertiveness, examples would be:

1. speaking up to friends and family

2. speaking up more each day little by little

3. public speaking in small groups

4. public speaking in large groups

5. speaking up to someone belligerent or annoying

6. stopping someone belligerent or annoying

7. stopping a physical bully

8. stopping an emotional bully

9. defending a point of view

10. defending yourself from verbal attack

Positive motivations include a friendly audience and a desire to please someone such as the opposite sex.

Some helpful pursuits are:

1. sports

2. relationships, loving others

3. fitness, strength and endurance

4. relaxation

5. defiance of emotions such as anger, increased information about the subject, sense of safety and challenging yourself to do more and more to face fears.

Focus on other people's needs and concerns and try to appear calm for self-respect and respect ot others.

Imagine being a superhero, with special kinds of powers. For example, the incredible hulk, a 7 ft. 500 lb. Green skinned monster who can lift 100,000 pounds and leap three miles, driven by rage.

A good luck charm, such as a cross or mezuzah may help. Also, confidence that the situation will turn out right helps.

Another helpful idea is being unconventional, not part of the "in" crowd who do not like altruistic, heroic actions. To be a hero, one must notice an event, understand that it is urgent, assume responsibility, know the type of aid to deliver, and finally decide to act. Do not view failure as a catastrophe, instead be willing to fail. For example, when I was young and coming home from work one night, I saw a man running along the subway platform. I thought nothing of it until I saw two policemen sprinting after him about later. If I had tackled him as I had done in football, I would have been a hero. Other times, I received a pat on the back from police for saving lives.

The difference between heroism and altruism is one of degree. The act of being steady in enduring danger or pain has no value unless it helps someone immediately or somewhere along the line. Some people do not value an activity unless there is danger or pain. This is wrong. Dr. Josephine Naidoo said that heroism is dependent on caring for others. She was right.

Other helpful ideas are, exercise, work, meditation, relaxation, socializing with signicant others, adventure-readiness and recreation as well as pleasure to rest our will power muscle. Visualization, prayer, self-hypnosis, caring, confidence and CBT also help.

Remember that discretion is the better part of valor. Muhammad Ali, said you can't be brave without fear. He meant that people without fear are missing something and absence of fear is not a virtue. He knew.

The courage quotient or functional courage is willingness to act divided by level of anxiety.

Another important aspect of spiritual fitness is getting along well with your deity, yourself, and your fellow man as well as the creatures of the earth. It is a matter of having good moral principles and following them. Personally, I believe in following most of the ten commandments, most of the Jewish tenets that I grew up in and as are roughly outlined in the Old Testament. I have also added the Quaker belief of not using violence on someone and that the light of God shines in everyone, including myself, so we respect it.

I believe in doing the right thing for the right reason and having physical, personal, and moral courage. Personal courage is a matter of triumphing in man versus himself conflicts. Moral courage is a matter of having moral principles, following them and standing up for them. Physical courage is steady in man versus nature. I believe in aspiring to a life of heart-filled integrity. Spiritual fitness put mind and soul into peak condition.

It involves kindness, love for fellow man and God. It is dealing with people honestly and developing healthy, loving relationships with people. Meditation is helpful, especially done everyday. Finding your purpose is helpful and involves examining your values to find out what you want to do.

Emotional Fitness

The usefulness of multi-faceted fitness is to have self-control, spontaneity, and independence. Self-control is a matter of being in control of our own actions. Spontaneity is that our actions come of our own accord. Independence is a matter of making our own decisions and taking responsibility for them.

An emotionally fit person can assess himself honestly, his strengths and weaknesses and feel good about them. We must play up our strengths, downplay our weaknesses, and feel good about our strengths. We must recognize the same in others and treat them the same. He acceps his part in family, organizations, society, world and universe.

We must make our own decisions, own opinions, own thoughts, feelings, behaviour and take responsibility for their consequences. Make the most of yourself and your situation and do the same for others. Be constructive about yourself and others. Self-control, spontaneity, and independence are important. Independence is not feeling controlled by others.

One should be present-centred and process-absorbed, absorbed in the process before them, enjoying life to the fullest. Be forward-looking, positive and optimistic.

Doing something you do not want to do, or not doing something you want to do will make you sick to a large extent. Feel good, think well, good mood, and good actions are important. Live by your own rules, values, and attitudes.

One must have pleasant, healthy emotions such as enjoyment, love, calmness and freedom from fear and anger. There is no emotion that will drive up blood pressure like anger. If you get angry, you must try to get over it as soon as possible. Try to express it in a constructive way and forget about it. Tell people how their actions make you feel and go on to doing something that you want to do. In order to have pleasant emotions, you must have work that you want to do, have hobbies and recreation that you enjoy and surround yourself with people that give you love, affection, and nurturance.

Another part of emotional fitness is loving yourself and others. Once you love yourself, you become open to loving others. Loving yourself is called self-esteem. You must take satisfaction with what you do and who you are. However, you must remember that everyone is important without conditions attached to it. Having self-esteem is a matter of how you talk to yourself. Monitor what you say to yourself and get rid of statements like I am no good, I am evil, I am incompetent, etc. Substitute statements like I am good, I am useful, I am warm etc.

Independence is a matter of not needing anyone, meaning absolutely no one in any way. The idea that we need other people is a myth. It may be nice to deal with people, but we should not need them. We must respect ourselves, have confidence in ourselves and have our opinions, and realize that if we have a problem that the only helping hand that we can rely on is the one at the end of our sleeve.

In order to control our thoughts, our conscious mind and higher mental centres is the general and the subconscious mind is the foot soldiers. Both are important, but the general is the most important part of the army. The subconscious does the fighting, but the general controls it.

We must realize that all people have similarities and differences, but no two people are even close to being exactly alike. Do not think you can be exactly like someone else and do not compare yourself to others. Also, no one activity can be our salvation as no one activity can be our downfall.

We must filter out bad ideas and only use the good ones. Take the best and leave the rest. There is no one idea, belief, philosophy, or anything that is a panacea. Also, especially, no one person or even anyone can be relied on completely, as no one person should be considered totally bad and totally toxic.

The doctor who caused my schizophrenia said that schizophrenia is a disease of lack of socialization. That is baloney. In fact, it is forced socialization that caused my schizophrenia.

If someone helps you, do not think that you owe them too much. This idea can be very dangerous and lead to excessive dependence on people.

Also, the idea of a certain abominable sin that makes someone not deserve to live or live in society is wrong and disgusting. People who espouse that belief are self-righteous hypocrites, which are similar to psychopaths.

Conscience is the main source of our sense of responsibility and so is a main source of maturity. However, excessive anything is bad.

The idea of genetically inferior, or inherently bad is a myth. This idea was espoused by my family and the doctor who caused my schizophrenia. Usually that only applies to psychopaths. GI is the term they applied to me.

The esteem of others, or admiration, is basically a want, rather than a need. Self-esteem deficits cause schizophrenics' delusions of grandeur, which makes them seem arrogant and conceited

All or none attitudes, that are a problem of both Diana Nyad, myself and other very aggressive people are bad as is extremity and can lead to failure and danger.

The idea that there are certain tight gender roles or characteristics is also very toxic and wrong. Assuming a characteristic to any group is wrong, both morally and factually. Trying to prove something in the past by comparing it to the present is also wrong morally and factually.

The idea that very aggressive people need something to hate and become bigots is dangerously wrong. Bigots, like Adolph Hitler, Hermann Goering, and Harry Beer are mostly pathological personalities. Others are ignorant or just want to hate. Less aggressive people I know hate just as much as very aggressive people. They have small consciences.

The idea of absoluteness is also wrong. The belief that we can start completely new is also wrong, especially as we get older.

The fear of death is part of our survival instincts. Someone without it is in trouble and the idea of a courageous death is a myth. Even mosquitoes die gracefully. However, fear of death is not realistic because all living things die.

The idea that we can or must be totally honest is not realistic.

If people can build you up or tear you down, you are in trouble. The idea that what people think of you is none of your business is a good one.

The idea that certain activities or people are inherently immoral or bad when they do not harm anyone is wrong and detrimental to our mental health. Be true to yourself and follow your own heart.

Do not put excessive value on courage and heroism. They go against our survival instincts and obsessions are bad.

You do not have to remember your origins or favors from the past.

Our thoughts do not matter. It is what you say or do that matters, especially what we do. In the end it is between us and God and not between us and other people. Only God can read our minds and evaluate our intentions and behaviour. Trying to explain behavious is like trying to smell the number nine.

At the same time that we do not need other people, we do not heal in isolation because most of our behaviour is based on interactions with other people. However, the idea that we need other people or that socialization is a virtue and lack of it is bad is the one that I have found destructive to good relationships and is part of my schizophrenia.

Relying on ourselves for everything, including contact with other people also helps us to be emotionally independent. We do what we want and believe what we want that way.

Intellectual Fitness

Intellectual fitness is a matter of discovering your intellectual capabilities and using them to their utmost to make the most of yourself. Personally, I do not learn very well, so I write. My PhD is in writing rather than academic learning.

Another person may have a great ability to learn, as I once did. We must exercise our intellectual capacities and use them. Brain exercises, reading, and writing help as does keeping a journal. All six aspects of fitness are inter-related. By developing one, we improve the other five. By developing all six, we make ourselves multi-faceted diamonds, with much to offer the world.

Someone with just an average I.Q. Can go on to get straight As in university as I did. I did it by working hard, using every minute of the day. I organized my work so that I would write out and repeat everything I needed to know several times ad infinitum. When I had an essay to do, I got it done well in advance. I collected all the facts that I could, then organized them so that all the parts of the essay would fit together. I left no stone unturned in doing the research. When I went from one class to another, I would review material that I needed to know. When I listened to a teacher lecture, I would put other thoughts on the back burner and give the teacher my undivided attention. I would be thinking about how I could use the material he gave us and form opinions on what he said. I would ask questions and make up questions that the teacher would answer in his class. I was curious to learn as much as possible. I took thorough notes on all that was useful. When I took a test, I had confidence that I knew what I had to know and could not learn it any better.

However, eventually the cognitive deficit got worse because what the medication was doing for me did not last more than seven years. I had to leave nursing school because of that and could never learn much after that. I had to get around the cognitive deficit by doing other things such as writing.

Physical Fitness

Physical fitness is a state in which one feels good and his body can do what it wants and does not pose a concern for him. More will be said about this in other parts of the book on physical health.

Financial Fitness

Financial fitness is something that I am not an expert on, but it is still very important. It is important to plan ahead and save money as well as possible for when you need it.

Financial fitness has three aspects. One is saving and conserving. The other is making money and the other is investing money. I will now present about 120 ways to do this.

1. Pick a bank that gives back. Seek out perks like no ATM fees, high interest on savings accounts, and no overdraft fees.

2. Divide up your paycheck. Put a specific amount into your savings account each check so that you will not be inclined to touch it.

3. Set financial goals.

4. Monitor your account like a hawk so that you see that it is doing alright.

5. Use debit cards sparingly and avoid ATMs that charge.

6. Plan withdrawals from the bank to limit fees.

7. Get your hair done for free at schools or low price.

8. Stay healthy.

9. Give up expensive habits.

10. Avoid copayments

11. Make your own shaving cream.

12. Use heat and air conditioning as little as possible.

13. Insulate your home.

14. Stay warm with blankets and clothes, not heat.

15. Use television sparingly.

16. Ditch cable.

17. Use energy efficient bulbs.

18. Unplug devices when you're not using them.

19. Make your own greeting cards.

20. Use the library for most reading needs

21. Use theater and entertainment at cheap times.

22. Check newspaper for cheap events.

23. Make your own gifts.

24. Have some picnics.

25. Organize your home and closet.

26. Check labels. Avoid dry cleaning.

27. Take care of your clothes.

28. Sniff your laundry to see if it is really necessary.

29. Leave your wallet at home so you will not be tempted to use it.

30. Use cold water to wash clothes.

31. Use coupons.

32. Wait for sales.

33. Buy generic.

34. Holiday shop after the holidays. Look for bargains.

35. When you see something you want, put off buying for thirty days.

36. Buy in bulk.

37. Grow your own food.

38. Write a shopping list and stick to it.

39. Scrutinize grocery bargains.

40. Go grocery shopping on a full stomach and alone.

41. Bring your own bag to shopping.

42. Buy in season.

43. Choose organic only some of the time.

44. Ask for rain checks.

45. Avoid checkout line fare.

46. Drink more water from the tap and avoid soda and juice.

47. Eat frozen vegetables.

48. Cook multiple meals at once.

49. Make your own coffee.

50. Save every nickel you can.

51. Brown bag lunch.

52. Make your own snacks.

53. Understand expiration dates to prevent food spoilage.

54. Stay vegetarian as much as possible.

55. Store dry goods and freeze them.

56. Walk and bike whenever possible.

57. Use public transportation.

58. When investing start with safe, lower yield products, then move to higher yield, more risk, when you have more money.

59. Spend less.

60. Have a good interest savings account stack.

61. Invest windfalls, eg 5,000 dollar bonuses in a 7% interest fund.

62. Limit investment trades.

63. Monitor money and credit.

64. Use Fidelity high yield mutual funds.

65. Save directly sometimes if you do not have enough money to invest.

66. Do not invest or buy when you do not feel good.

67. Focus first on more short-term financial goals. Invest for the future when you have enough.

68. Pay as little tax as possible.

69. Protect the principal of your investments.

70. Look to how much income your nest egg will earn at retirement.

71. Take investment courses, especially real estate.

72. Invest in Facebook and Linkedin stocks.

73. Save money by selling an expensive condo for a cheaper one.

74. Earn real estate rental income.

75. Sometimes slow return is good.

76. Save for the future and rainy days.

77. Invest in high yield bonds.

78. Diversify your investment portfolio.

79. Don't keep bad investments or expenses.

80. Move to a cheaper place.

81. Live in a cheap town.

82. Monitor expenses and budget.

83. Pay yourself savings first just like you would a bill.

84. Collect your small change, not squander it.

85. Bank your refunds and save.

86. Continue paying off a loan.

87. Get rid of costly habits, like buying breakfast and lunch.

88. No useless spending. Ask yourself why you are buying something and if no good reason do not buy, especially if you are depressed.

89. Crash save for 2-3 months, buy only absolute necessities.

90. Save expense account reimbursement money.

91. Keep your non-interest account balances to a minimum.

92. Pay off debt as soon as possible.

93. Do not buy on impulse, credit or not feeling good.

94. Wait for bargains.

95. Do not buy love or power.

96. Comparison shop. Buy generic.

97. No time-saving convenience foods.

98. Don't buy for status.

99. Keep nonfat dry milk on hand.

100. Stick to shopping lists.

101. Stock up on fruits or vegetables in season and freeze.

102. Do not be blindly faithful.

103. Hunt, fish, or grow your own food.

104. Buy food in bulk.

105. Only cook what you need.

106. Use discount stores for clothing and wear your good clothes seldom.

107. Try cutting your own hair.

108. Attend low cost matinees and entertainment.

109. Sell off what you no longer need.

110. Care for items you own so you don't have to replace them.

111. You can't take it with you. Be wary of estate planning expenses.

112. Look for ways to make money like selling books, magazine articles, and other goods and services you produce.

113. Look for ways to develop new skills to earn money.

114. Get advice on money from someone you trust.

115. Concoct your own cleaning solution with vinegar, olive oil, and baking soda.

Physical Fitness

Level 1 – Heavy limbs – weights on ankles and wrists – start with 1 lb. To 3 lbs. To 5 lbs. And later 10 lbs. Lift knee and hand together with weights and alternate other side for 10 minutes.

Burpees on a bench – stand up straight, bend down to put hands on bench, push legs out and return for 2 minutes.

Sprints on bench – hands on bench, alternate position of legs from front to back.

Dry land swim – on bench when prone, standing, or sitting.

Walk, swim, or sport for 10-20 minutes each day or more.

Two times per week -

Lift weights – curls with back against wall with dumbbells.

Shoulder presses with dumbbells.

Press backwards with dumbbells, felt in tricep

Upright rows with dumbbells.

Neck shrugs, dumbbells in hands at sides.

Shoulder row with one hand on bench, one arm, one dumbbell at a time.

Elbows high, hands with dumbbells overhead, arms straight, drop hands backwards to shoulders and back up again.

Bench press or pushups.

Situps or crunches

Toe or ground touches and alternate toe touches to alternate feet.

Level 2 – Marathons

1. Swim 300 yards in 10 minutes, five to six days per week. Add 20 yards per day within tolerance. Continue for four weeks.

2. Substitute one 900 to 1000 yard swim for one 300 yard swim.

3. Substitute two 900 to 1000 yard swims for two 300 yard swims. Work up to two 1400 yard swims.

4. Do two 1800 plus yards swims plus other 300 plus yards swims.

5. Build up to 1800 yards swims five to six times per week.

6. Continue for four weeks and add 100 yards per week.

7. Add one two mile swim for one time per week.

8. Add one one and one half mile swim one time per week.

9. Work up to two miles per day.

10. Work up to three miles per day.

11. Continue for one month.

12. Work up to ten miles swim one time per week.

13. Add 100 to 200 yards to shorter swims plus one quarter to one half miles to the longer swim so that you are eventually doing five miles shorter swims and 18 miles longer swims.

14. Add one mile to longer swim to 26 miles then to 32 miles.

This program is based on the idea that you can swim three times your average for the last month or three months.

For running marathons or ultra-marathons, distance is same. Running four mile is the equivalent of swimming one mile.

Isometrics

Isometrics pit one muscle against the other or one muscle against an immovable object. Following are some exercises:

1. neck pushes with hands against front, back, and sides.

2. Arms in front squeeze hands together

3. push against sides of knees

4. back to wall, press hands against wall with triceps.

5. Press down on knees

6. Shoulder shrug on chair.

7. Biceps curl

8. sit ups

9. squeeze rubber balls

10. press down on chair

11. hands over head squeeze

12. rope pull apart and resist, hands at belly

13. belly press inward with hands

14. pull towel apart, hands overhead

15. pull towel apart, arms straight, at chest level

16. pull towel apart, belly level

17. pull towel apart, hands behind you

18. resist hand near head, both hands, pull on bicep

19. hands press on side of door

20. squeeze books

21. try to bend steel bar

22. cock wrists both ways

23. resistance against fingertips

24. fingertip pushups

25. lock fingers and push hands together

26. rip phone book or thick books

27. tear pack of cards

28. wrist roll with weights

29. chair lift with one hand

30. lever bar lift

31. pinch gripping weights

32. feet on chair hands on ground, pull abdomen in

33. lying leg press with towel

34. seated leg press with towel

35. quadriceps pull with towel

36. seated leg press together

37. wall squat

38. wall squat one legged

39. supine back extension

Dumbbell Weights

1. curls

2. shoulder press

3. triceps press – kickback

4. upright rows

5. shoulder shrugs

6. triceps press from shoulders

7. bent-over row

8. bench press or pushup

9. crunches

10. toe touch

11. kneeling curls

12. seated curls

13. concentration curls

14. prone curl

15. kickback – one dumbbell

16. lying triceps kickback – one dumbbell

17. bent over kickback

18. row kickback

19. lying extensions – bent arm plus straight arm

20. As above with one arm at a time-saving

21. French press – one dumbbell two hands

22. seated French press

23. one arm extensions

24. seated one arm extensions

25. lie on bench and row

26. prone lateral flies

27. prone lateral flies plus row

28. lying chest fly

29. chest fly on floor

30. decline or incline pushup

31. bent over raise for shoulders

32. front raise

33. wood chop

34. golf swing

35. weighted punch

Bodyweight Exercises

1. pull up

2. chins

3. ground – supine pulls between chairs with stick

4. one arm pushup

5. one arm pushup hold

6. full bridge

7. overhead leg extensions

8. triceps pushups

9. incline pushups

10. decline pushups

11. triceps pushups

12. headstand to handstand with two arms and one arm

13. rotating T pushup

14. downward dog

15. spider pushup

16. side to side pushup

Handbalancing

Learn to handbalance by practicing against a wall. Place your hands on the floor shoulder width apart and about 18 inches from a flat wall. Keep your fingers pointing towards the wall and spread them wide apart, in order to give you the biggest possible base for a handstand. Look at the wall where it meets the floor, lean your body forward and, keeping your arms straight, kick your legs up and overhead until your heels strike the wall.

When your heels strike the wall above you stretch your toes up high and raise your head slowly until your heels come away from the wall. Try to hold this position as long as possible. If your heels touch the wall again, then repeat the stretching and head raising. If your legs come down to the floor, then kick them up to the wall again. This is the best way to learn to do a handstand. For a handbalance walk, simply overbalance and compensate by taking a step with your hands.

Stretching

1. feet backward and up while standing

2. toe touches

3. ankle rotations

4. elbows up and back – touch upper back with fingers

5. arms and hips to side while standing

6. wrist extensor stretch and opposite way wrist back

7. wrist flexor stretch – move wrist forward.

Social Fitness

Social fitness allows you to deal with people and is very important.

Try and talk to people, and maybe you will find That underneath their quiet reserve, they're really very kind. Remember, people are often shy and sometimes not too sure, but very ready to respond to a friendly overture. There really is no telling where such talk will end. You may be quite surprised to find that you have made a friend.

Social fitness consists of having some close friends, being able to work with and get along with people, being assertive, and being able to influence people favorably at times.

I have found that being friendly and helpful is very important. I am always willing to do someone a favor, if he or she really needs it and is not taking advantage. In order to have friends, you need to talk to people, express your liking for them and get to know them better. Share ideas, thoughts, feelings and generally help each other.

The rules for developing friendships with the opposite sex are the same. First, you must be with people you want to meet. Go to places where other people share the same interests. When you see someone you like, meditate on him or her and decide what it is you like about this person. Approximately one person in every ten, on average is a good match. Again, share things that you have in common – thoughts, ideas, feelings etc. and share good times together. Help each other and you may find someone that you want to marry.

In order to get along with people at work, you must be friendly, helpful, and assertive. If someone steps on you, you must let him know how it makes you feel. This will save you a lot of grief. You must be able to appreciate a favor someone does for you and not expect it. You must expect nothing from anyone, including the fact that if people can build you up or tear you down, you are in trouble.

Assertive communication is a matter of saying what's on your mind, saying what you mean and meaning what you say and helping others do the same. You must know your own worth and that of others, be clear about your goals, be prepared to learn from successes and failures and be flexible and not expect too much. Learning to listen is one of the most important skills. You must know your own worth, have mutual respect, accept yourself and others for who you are and give yourself to succeed and fail.

It is important to stand up for human rights. Human rights are everybody's worth. We all have the right to choose. We all have the right to exist. We all have the right to be respected. We all have the right to make mistakes. We all have the right to say no. We all have the right to ask for what we want and for what we need. A Nazi principal that I once had who pretended hypocritically to be a Quaker violated all these rights and was extremely violent. His name was Harry Beer and was a sociopath, like most Nazis.

In order to rid fear, we must understand our fears and accept ourselves for who we are. In the main we are what we are supposed to be, where we are supposed to be, and doing what we are supposed to be doing.

Release all your disappointments and guilty feelings. Forgive yourself. Everything you have done and experienced has brought you to this point of change. If you want to change and decide to change, here are some helpful ideas.

Project forward in time and imagine how you would look and feel if you were in control of the communication. Compare this to how you feel now. Imaging and visualizing are useful tools. By "bringing to mind," or "picturing in your mind's eye," your desired state you are actually putting images into your subconscious that help to improve your behaviour. Your subconscious is like the army full of soldiers, governed by lower centres in the brain and the conscious mind is the general who ultimately makes decisions, governed by higher centres in the brain, but cannot do everything by himself. Old habits die hard, but they do die. Give yourself permission to succeed and fail, and be dispassionate with these two conditions. There are only learning experiences. It is not always easy, but rewarding. Create winning scenarios.

Conversations

The most important part of conversations is active listening. 82 % of people would rather talk to a great listener than a great speaker. Active listening means concentration, full attention, non-verbal feedback such as nodding the head and forward lean and verbal feedback such as yeah, good, mmmhmm. Also positive reinforcement such as yes or indeed, asking relevant questions and making statements that help to build or clarify what the speaker has said are helpful. One should reflect and repeat, clarify, and summarize what the person has said. Asking relevant questions is also helpful.

In starting conversations, we must choose the right time and place, say Hi, choose the topic, and judge interest. If there is no interest move on rather than pushing yourself onto someone. Some topics include pets, family, sports, hobbies, groups, clubs, jobs and schools.

Put yourself in the other's mindset. Give more than you get. Bring up friend's favorite subjects.

There are six C's of comfortable conversation. One is compliment, two is courtesy, three is common interest, four is complaint, five is circumstances such as the environment, and six is convenience.

In connecting with people, everyone's favorite subject is themselves. Take clues and put yourself in the other person's shoes. Ask sensitive questions. For example, where do you live? Ask someone's last few hours. This works well with both friends and strangers. Ask what time they woke up. Ask what challenges they faced at work, or where they had lunch and with whom.

In making a friendship with complete strangers, bring up any subject that you can logically follow with another question. For example, you can ask where to buy something, where restaurants, movies, home computers or other things are. Then you can follow up and say that you forget where to buy it. You can call to thank them later on.

The next step is to ask them about their interests. Also, you can give people a complimentary nickname such as something about what they do. For instance, someone who helps you medically can be Dr. Camille, or someone who teaches you can be professor. Good doers can be Saint Stephanie, or Archangel Gabriel.

Get people to articulate their attitudes. Become opinionated. Take a stand on possible subjects you think about. Be passionate. When in Rome do as the Romans do. Match your words to your audience. Cover up the embarrassment of others. Never change a subject someone finds special.

An example of a conversation starter is to ask how a couple first met. Ask line of work. What would a typical day look like. How did you get the job and why?

Expand on compliments and go on and on as long as possible. Ask your partner what they are most proud of. Praise and praise publicly.

Do not criticize, condemn, or complain. Give honest and sincere appreciation. Arouse in the other person an eager want by dangling a reward in front of them and giving them a small sample of it to whet their appetite. Other rules for dealing with people are:

1. Become genuinely interested in people like a dog to its master. It wags its tail and gets excited when it sees him.

2. Smile

3. Call people by name.

4. Be a good listener. Encourage others to talk about themselves.

5. Talk in terms of the other person's interests.

6. Be sincere in the way in which you make the other person feel important.

7. Avoid arguments completely.

8. Show respect for other people's opinions. Never say, "You're wrong."

9. If you are wrong, admit it quickly and emphatically.

10. Explain your point of view in a friendly way.

11. Emphasize your similarities first.

12. Let the other person do a great deal of the talking.

13. Let the other person feel that an idea is his or hers.

14. Sincerely try to see things from the other person's point of view.

15. Be sympathetic to the other person's ideas and desires. Say things like, I don't blame you one bit.

16. Appeal to peoples' nobler motives. People want to feel that they are great, idealistic, honest, upright and fair.

17. Present facts in bold, dramatic, creative ways. This can be very difficult.

18. Throw down challenges to people like, "Try to beat this."

19. Begin criticism with honest praise and appreciation, then give the beef, then more honest praise.

20. Be subtle and indirect when pointing out mistakes.

21. Talk about your own mistakes first before mentioning the other person's goof.

22. Ask questions in order to give suggestions, not orders. People do not like to take orders.

23. Give people dignity and do not embarrass them.

24. When people show the slightest improvement, be lavish with praise and reward.

25. Give people a good name and reputation to live up to.

26. Make a fault seem easy to correct. Do not criticize the person, just a minor glitch. Use encouragement.

27. Make the person feel important by suggesting a task that he is the best man for the job.

When trying to persuade someone, be sincere. Do not promise anything you cannot deliver. Concentrate on benefits to the other person and forget about benefits to yourself. Ask the other person what he really wants and consider the benefits to the other person if he does what you suggest. Match these benefits to the person's wants, such as being a great employee making a good company image.

These principles are what made Reverend Harry Martin and Dorothy Leslie, RN such excellent supervisors and a delight to work for. About the other supervisors who did not follow these principles, the less said, the better.

When talking to someone, lean forward, and try to catch every word they say, touch them appropriately, make eye contact, smile, and have an open posture. Also nod your head in acknowledgement at times.

When talking to strangers, often boldness is your best friend. A woman met me by walking up to me, putting her hand in mine, and asking, "Do you want to live together?"

I said, "Yes."

Now, she is my wife.

I have a story about a raccoon who was trapped on an eavestrough and was wet and uncomfortable. A flock of birds flying overhead covered his body with excrement, which kept him warm. Because he was making noises showing his discomfort with having excrement on him, a passerby hosed it off. Now he was much more uncomfortable.

The moral of the story is that somebody who gets you into excrement is not necessarily your enemy. Somebody who gets you out of excrement is not necessarily your friend, and if you're happy in excrement, shut up about it.

BRAIN CARE AND SLEEP CARE

For sleep care here are some suggestions:

1. Sleep in a comfortable bed.

2. Sleep in a dark, quiet room at a comfortable temperature.

3. Arise and go to bed at the same times each day.

4. Get regular exercise, eat a healthy diet and keep fit.

5. Get outdoor sunlight at the same time each day.

6. Take a warm bath, a milky drink, eat oatmeal, read, listen to quiet music, visualize pleasant scenes, relaxation exercises or listen to a monotone tape.

7. Use melatonin sometimes.

8. Use thought stopping of bad thoughts.

9. Use bedroom for sleep and sex only.

10. Get up after half an hour if you cannot sleep.

11. Avoid anything stimulating before bed

12. Avoid heavy or spicy meals before bed.

13. Do not check the clock.

14. Have a relaxing sleep ritual.

15. Restrict time in bed.

16. Avoid or cope with stress.

17. Keep a sleep diary and thoughts about sleep.

18. Use guided imagery.

19. Empty your mind of disruptive thoughts.

20. Focus on inconsequential things.

21. Cuddle your partner or have sex before bed.

22. Try traditional Chinese medicine.

23. Try acupressure or self-massage.

24. Try biofeedback.

25. Use yoga and stretching.

26. Experiment with different sleep positions.

27. Journal positive things.

28. Self-hypnosis.

29. Tai Chi

30. Have a peaceful hour before bed and wind down.

31. Focus on breathing and slow breathing to 2-6 breaths per minute.

For brain care look up Daniel Amen, Norman Doidge, Michael Sweeney and do their brain exercises. You can find them at Amazon.com or Amazon.ca. That will give more on brain care than I can, other than my section on intellectual fitness, as well as my total plan with six points and sixteen point acronym, Boldly Travel Hero.

ORAL SUPPLEMENTATION

Regular oral supplementation should be conservative and should contain half a multi-vitamin containing the following nutrients:

1. vitamin A – 2,500 IU

2. B1 – 25 mg.

3. B2 – 25 mg.

4. B3 – 100 mg.

5. B5 – 300 mg.

6. B6 – 4 mg.

7. B9 – 400 mg. From methylfolate

8. B12 -25 mg.

9. Biotin – 300 mg.

10. Vitamin C – 1,000 mg.

11. D – 1,000 mg.

12. E – 400IU

13. lycopene – 400 mg.

14. Lutein – 40 mg.

15. Quercetin -

16. Omega 3 – 900 mg. DHA 1-3 times daily

17. cinammon - 1 teaspoon daily

18. saw palmetto for men

19. red pepper or capsaicin to suppress appetite

20. turmeric

21. zeaxanthin – 2 mg. Per day.

22. Co Q 10 – 200 mg. Per day

23. coffee or green tea – 2 or more cups per day

24. probiotics - 4 billion cells of healthy gut bacteria

More will be added on supplements in the section on blood vessels.

LESS FOOD

It was found that the less food that laboratory rats ate, the healthier they were and the longer they lived, by a factor of 50%. It is recommended that most people cut back their food intake by 15%.

A protein called surtuin enables improved health and is secreted with caloric restriction. It calms cell division so that younger cells proliferate and become more numerous. Also, all systems function better on caloric restriction. One should eat enough to give energy. For dieting, usually 1400 calories are recommended. Eight glasses water at least are recommended. To break down the sample diet, 500 calories grains are used, then 100 calories vegetables, 120 calories fruits, 100 calories dairy, 300 calories protein, 200 calories fats, and 80 calories extras. Exercise is, of course, recommended.

Grains	100 calories each
Vegetables	30 calories each
Fruit	60 calories each
Dairy	60 calories each
Protein	150 calories each
Fats	100 calories each
Extras	
Fluids	
Exercise	

DIET

A low fat, low cholesterol diet consisting mainly of fruits and vegetables, presented here is best. Fruits and vegetables are nutritional powerhouses and one cannot go wrong with them.

I will now relate my experience with diet and weight loss. I have been overweight at times in my life and have usually gotten my weight down. Too restrictive a diet can cause low blood sugar which makes someone angry and tense. One must be comfortably hungry all the time

One diet that I have found useful I call the hunger index diet. It consists of using your level of hunger to guide your food intake. One must eat just enough to keep up blood sugar. This ensures that we never become irritable or nervous. If I felt overly hungry, I would eat a healthy snack like a banana or an apple. I would finish eating a little hungry and keep my level of hunger at that point all day long. I found that I lost a pound every few days. I quickly lost 10 pounds. When I was satisfied with my weight, I would maintain it by eating just enough to satisfy myself and no more. If the weight would creep up, I would go back on the hunger index diet.

I also found a low-fat, low cholesterol, vegetarian diet helpful. This diet consisted of fruits, vegetables, fat-free yogurt and egg whites. The eggs are hard boiled, cut in half and the yolks are tossed. Fish or chicken can be eaten from time to time. This diet made me leaner and stronger than ever. A vegetarian diet helps you lose weight because it contains less calories and fat than other diets. You feel full, but have consumed less calories.

The basis of the hunger index diet is to eat when you need to rather than when you want to eat. It is helpful if you can start by writing down everything you eat, when you eat it and how you feel. You must accurately chart a nutrition profile of everything you eat using a food count book or MyFitnessPal.com. If you take in no more than

1300 to 1400 calories, you will learn to ignore false signals and only eat what you really need when you need it.

Vegetarian Food Groups

Grains – barley, bread, whole wheat, rye, pumpernickel, triticale, corn, pita, buckwheat berries and flour, cereals, cooked oatmeal, prepared granola, grape nuts, bulghur, corn, Kasha, oats, pasta, popcorn, rice soybeans

Legumes – aduki beans, bay beans, bean sprouts, bean flakes, black beans, brown beans, calico beans, cannelini or white beans, cowpeas, fava beans, chick peas, kidney beans, lentils, miso soup from soybeans, Navy beans, peas, pinto beans, red beans, soybeans, soy flour, soy grits, soy milk, split peas, tofu.

Vegetables – artichokes, asparagus, bamboo shoots, beets, beet greens, Belgian endive, broccoli, brussels sprouts, cabbage – common, Chinese, red, Savoy cabbage, bok choy, carrots, cauliflower, celery, chives, collards, cucumbers, escarole, garden cress, green beans, kale, kohlrabi, leeks, lettuce, lima beans, mushrooms, spinach, okra, onions, parsley, parsnips, potatoes, yams, pumpkin, radishes, rutabagas, turnip, summer squash, yellow zuchini, green zuchini, red, green and yellow peppers, Swiss chard, tomatoes, chestnuts, wax beans, winter squash, acorn squash, butternut squash.

Fruits – apples, apricots, bananas, blackberries, blueberries, cherries, cranberries, currants, dates, figs, gooseberries, grapefruit, grapes, lemons, limes, loganberries, mangoes, cantaloupes, honeydews, nectarines, oranges, papayas, peaches, pears, pineapples, plantain, plum, prunes, raisins, raspberries, strawberries, tangerines, watermelons,

Vegetable Stew Recipe

1. Combine garlic, leeks, celery, cut up vegetables and juice in a pot. The juice can be chicken broth, mango or papaya juice or tomato juice. Warm water can be used t9 keep stew moist.

2. Boil, then simmer for a few hours.

Add any vegetables or spices that please you, the more the better.

Egg White and Tomato Sandwich

Hard boil the eggs. Then cut them in half and remove the yolk. Serve with tomato, Dijon mustard and cucumber on whole wheat bread. Hummus can substitute for egg white.

Stuffed Green Peppers

Boil brown rice in tomato juice until soft. Add lentils and stuff the green pepper after cutting out the top. Bake on a 400 degree preheated oven until brown. Pour stewed tomatoes over the peppers before they cook. Add spices.

Cabbage Rolls

Stuff the cabbage leaves the way you stuffed the green peppers. Pour over stewed tomatoes and spices. Cook for an hour in a 400 degree preheated oven.

Multi-Grain Cereal

Combine six or twelve or more grains from a health food store and boil in water until cooked usually about 25 minutes. Three parts water to one part cereal.

Lentil Burgers

2/3 c. lentils

3c. Water

whole wheat bread crumbs one c.

½ c. wheat germ

½ c. chopped onion

4 raw egg whites

Cook lentils until soft. Mash in with remaining ingredients. Spray a pan with Pam and cook until golden brown and firm. Serve with bread and condiments.

Vegetarian Chili

1 c. onion

1c. parsley

11/2 c. potatoes, diced

1c. diced carrots

½ c. red pepper, diced

½ c. zuchini, diced

1c. cooked or canned kidney beans

2 T minced garlic

2 c. canned tomatoes

4T mild chili powder

¼ c. water

3c. cooked rice or corn

Add all ingredients. Simmer until crisp-tender about 30 min. to an hr. or more. Serve over rice or corn.

Lentil-Rice Curry

11/2c. Lentils

3c.water

2c. brown rice

4c. water

3c. chopped onion

Peter Cohen

1 chopped pepper

1 grated green apple

2 large cloves garlic, minced

2T curry powder

1/2t. Cumin 11/2 c. frozen peas

cayenne pepper

2T coriander plus raisins and Chutney

Cook lentils and rice in separate pots. Saute onion, pepper, apple, garlic, curry and cumin until soft. Add vegetable and peas to lentils Add cayenne and lemon. Add cucumber and coriander Serve over rice. Add chutney and raisins.

Hummus

1 can chick peas or lentils

6 cloves garlic

black and cayenne pepper

3T lemon juice

2T Dijon mustard

1t basil and oregano.

Combine food and mash or with a food processor or hand blender until soft.

Spicy Rice and Beans

2 cloves garlic, minced

1 onion

1 green pepper, cubed

1 zuchini, cubed

¾ c. brown rice

½ c. dried lentils, rinsed, drained

½ t. each chili powder, oregano

1/4t. Cumin

3c. chicken broth

1c. chunky salsa

1c.frozen corn

1 can red kidney beans plus pepper

Heat garlic and onion in water 3to5 min. until soft. Add green pepper and zuchini, cook 3 min. Stir in rice, lentils, chili powder, oregano and cumin, cook 1 min. Add stock, salsa, corn, kidney beans and pepper. Spoon mixture into 12 cup casserole. Bake, covered in a 350 degree oven 2 hours or until rice and lentils are tender.

Vegetable Soup

8 cups assorted vegetables

8 cups water

basil, oregano, marjoram and rosemary, cayenne and black pepper

Add whole wheat macaroni and lentils and cook for 20 minutes or until tender.

Oat Bran and Maple Muffins

2 c. oat bran

2t. baking powder

1t. cinammon

½ c. maple syrup

½ c. plain, nonfat yogurt

2 raw egg whites, separated

½ c. raisins.

Preheat oven to 400 degrees. Spray Pam on 12 cup muffin tin. In a bowl, combine oat bran, baking powder and cinammon. In another bowl combine remaining ingredients. Sir both bowls together. Pour into muffin tin. Bake until lightly brown and springy to touch. Cool before serving.

Spinach-Lentil Soup

1c.cooked lentils

1c. uncooked green split peas

1c. barley

7c. water

2 potatoes

2 onions

garlic powder

2t dill, chopped

1/2t. Chopped dill

1. Put the lentils, peas, barley and water into a pot and boil. Reduce heat and simmer another 25 minutes.

2. Rinse potatoes, dice unpeeled and cook in water to cover until they are firm.

3. Saute onion, garlic and pepper in a bit of water in a separate pot. When they are soft, add spinach slowly, after cleaning until it wilts, then add more.

4. Add all mixtures to the lentil mixture. Simmer for 30 minutes, stir often. Add vinegar to taste.

LESS TOXINS

In trying to decrease toxin exposure, here a some guidelines:

1. Watch out for toxic chemicals in food products. Read labels and especially avoid nitrates and nitrites.

2. Try to avoid pollution of the air and water, where possible.

3. Use natural cleaning products and foods.

4. Avoid artificially made foods, concentrate on produce, fruits, vegetables, and fish for food.

5. Sweat out toxins.

6. Drink lots of tap water. Avoid bottled water.

7. Limit sun exposure. Cover skin. Wear sunscreen. Check radon and use a dehumidifier to decrease mold.

8. Watch out for garden pesticides, herbicides and paint. Bring in fresh air. Avoid cars. Avoid strange smells, THC and LSD. Avoid artificial insect repellents.

YOUTH

Youthfulness is basically a matter of following the six aspects of fitness and good health practices. For one thing, we should boost our immune system and decrease sugar intake.

1. avoid smoke and pollution

2. eat phytonutrients like broccoli, cabbage, carrots, tomatoes, soy, fish oil, onions, apples, garlic, mushrooms, ginger, green tea, and brussels sprouts.

3. Take vitamins like A, B group, C, E, and zinc and selenium.

4. Take liver enzyme enhancers such as n-acetyl cysteine, glutathione, whey, turmeric, l-glutamine, milk thistle.

5. Take antioxidants such as pycnogenol, grape seed extract, alpha lipoic acid, co Q 10, and avoid excess alcohol.

6. Take beta-carotene.

7. Use good fats, monounsaturated and polyunsaturated.

8. Avoid nitrates, nitrites, and meats.

9. Use soy and genistein.

10. Use rosemary, ginger, licorice, sesame, cucumber, bee pollen, bee propolis, royal jelly, algae, seaweed, wheat grass, chlorella, chlorophyll, kelp, flaxseed, dandelion, parsley, rose hips, spinach, bilberry, lycopene, olives, garlic, probiotics, yogurt, pectin.

11. Avoid stress, do relaxation and exercise.

Five factors of aging are:

1.   Inflammation – caused by visceral (belly) fat putting out inflammatory hormones, smoking, lack of exercise, and stress.

2.   Oxidation – combatted by taking antioxidants like vitamin E, C and beta-carotene.

3.   Glycation – caused by too much sugar and impaired sugar metabolism.

4.   Methylation – which can be balanced by folic acid in eggs and seeds.

5.   Immune deficits – a strong immune system slows aging.

Other ways to combat aging are ridding bad habits, personal care, lots of water, keeping energy good, having a solid relationship, and never retiring.

NEW TECHNOLOGIES

New technologies that might be expected in the future are:

1. nanotechnotechnology and possibly tiny robots called nanobots.

2. Cancer cures.

3. Bioartificial kidneys.

4. Tissue engineering of organs.

5. Joint replacements.

6. Stem cell therapy, which is using immature cells that will grow into the desired cells, tissues, and organs.

7. Transcranial magnetic stimulation for schizophrenia and other mental disorders and electroconvulsive shock therapy for the same.

8. Positive addictions used scientifically.

9. New medications.

10. Bionic parts sensitive to nerve stimuli.

Ray Kurzweil originally said in his excellent book called Transcend, that eventually microscopic-sized robots called nanobots will be injected into the body and programmed to fix everything that can go wrong with us so that we can live to be five thousand years old and perhaps beyond. However, my own knowledge says that our "adaptation energy" to handle stress and our reproductive capacity of cells and our immune system wear out and we eventually die. No one has yet lived longer that 125 years. In other words, like all living things, we are made to die. I wish that great thinkers like Kurzweil were right, they have better minds than mine, but I just don't see it.

Following are some ideas that are useful.

1. The law of accelerating returns says that discoveries lead to an increased capacity to make discoveries, especially in artificial intelligence.

2. Increased telomerase increases the life of the cell.

According to Corey James Kiz in his book, The Future, there will be earlier diagnosis of disease, machine-based technologies and sensor units to monitor health. This will lead to portable ICUs. People will carry around EKG machines in their hands and be on top of their many problems.

Dr. E. Fuller Torrey, called the most famous psychiatrist in America, says that in 50 years, mental illness will not exist. He sees it as an infectious disease that can be vaccinated against. I think that is ridiculous. Schizophrenia is known as an excess of dopamine in the limbic system and bipolar disorder is an excess of serotonin in the brain. Insults to the brain and mind caused by stress and trauma trigger these. There will no doubt be better treatments and I see transcranial magnetic stimulation, magnetic seizure therapy, and PET scan biofeedback as among these.

Weight gain and obesity must be controlled, or children will be more disabled than their parents.

Francis Collins views knowledge of human genetics to allow drugs specially suited to each individual and be more effective. Also, nanotechnological delivery of medication will allow more targeted delivery of medication without side effects and better therapeutic effects.

According to Lewis Ignaus, nitric oxide will cure heart disease. I question this. Tissue engineering of bioartificial organs, such as the heart, will be done, using part human tissue, often the patients own tissue, and encapsulated in artificial materials, so that there is no rejection. Already, a bioartificial kidney has been transplanted into chimpanzees.

Replacing organs grown from our own stem cells, (immature precursors to cells) may be routine.

Another therapy that may arise is somatic gene therapy. They will infect genes with new DNA and correct disease.

Also, a drug called Torcetratib blocks enzyme breaking down HDL and increases HDL cholesterol., which helps prevent heart disease.

The Future of Kidney-Failure Research

The future of kidney failure research is rapidly becoming the present. John Woods and David Humes are developing a bioartificial kidney that will one day do what a normal kidney does and will effectively be a cure for kidney failure. This research could take two years or more, but looks very promising. There are other areas of research, but they are not as promising as these two researchers at the University of Michigan.

There are several reasons why a bioartificial kidney is needed. Among them are the facts that current treatments have their many problems associated with them. For example:

1. Dialysis does not relieve symptoms completely.

2. Dialysis is sometimes painful.

3. Dialysis patients must restrict their fluid intake.

4. Dialysis is time consuming.

5. If someone is unable to get to dialysis for too long, he will die.

6. Restless people risk bleeding to death if they cannot sit still.

7. Dialysis patients must watch their potassium and phosphate intake.

8. Dialysis patients have problems such as clotted vascular access, catheter sepsis, and painful declotting procedures.

9. Dialysis patients must take many medications in order to replace what their failed kidneys do not do.

10. Kidney transplants require anti-rejection drugs that damage the body.

11. A transplanted kidney only lasts eight to ten years.

12. Some people have their transplanted kidneys fail after two or three years causing great psychological problems.

13. Being a transplant or dialysis patient causes psychological problems.

14. People on dialysis cannot vacation unless they are rich enough to afford dialysis away from home.

15. Kidney transplant patients are put through rigorous post-operative procedures such as having tubes run in and out of their bodies.

16. There is a lack of availability of suitable donor kidneys for transplant.

17. Dialysis does not replace calcitriol to control calcium balance. It gives limited excretion of potassium causing a need for dietary restriction. It is an ordeal and does not control blood pressure or metabolism and it does not produce hormones. Patients on dialysis have major problems. (Schnermann, 1994 pp. 1-201).

What An Ideal Bioartificial Kidney Will Do

An ideal bioartificial kidney would filter out harmful substances in the blood so that the body is detoxified of substances such as urea and creatinine. It would maintain water balance in the body. It would secrete necessary hormones such as erythropoietin, renin, and angiotensin and excrete excesses of sugar, drugs, and other substances such as amino acids and organic positively and negatively charged particles. It would control thirst and allow unrestricted fluid intake. It would also control the acid-base balance of the blood by excreting excess hydrogen ions and slowing down bicarbonate excretion, if necessary or doing the opposite if necessary. It would excrete excess sodium chloride (salt) and control sodium balance in the body as well as blood pressure. Above all, the patient could start urinating again, and the bioartificial kidney would last, hopefully, for the rest of the patient's long life span.

An ideal bioartificial kidney would bolster the patient's immune system to prevent destruction of white blood cells as well as allow the patient to have more energy. There would be less susceptibility to infection that is common among both kidney transplant recipients and dialysis patients.

Are these goals feasible? I think that they are. David Humes has replaced the kidneys of small animals with bioartificial kidneys that do most or all of what a real kidney can do. Dr. Humes assistant says that the bioartificial kidney must now be scaled up to implant into humans. After five years of testing, if it is successful, mass production will be possible (taken from a recording from Dr. Humes' lab). The University of Michigan is the only place where research into a bioartificial kidney is being conducted. University of Toronto is looking into tissue engineering of a bioartificial heart.

How Will Bioartificial Kidneys Be Made?

Bioartificial kidneys will be made by a process called tissue engineering. This is done by using materials and devices capable of specific interaction with biological tissues. These combine novel materials with living cells to yield functional tissue equivalents (University of Toronto, p.1). These tissues are useful for organ tissue replacement where there is a limited availability of donor organs, or where, in some cases, like nerves no natural replacements are available. These constructs are also useful for the delivery of gene therapy. This would be very useful for diabetics because genetic disorders often cause diabetes which often causes kidney failure. Tissue engineering can come in two guises: in one case cells are grown in culture and seeded onto a material, in another case an implanted material induces a specific response, such as tissue regeneration in living organisms (UofT p.1).

Tissue engineering exploits advances in a number of technologies such as: biomaterials, drug delivery, recombinant DNA techniques in which hereditary material, DNA is grown and alters the growth of living cells, biodegradable polymers, in which chemicals essential for life are broken down into their constituent parts, stem cell isolation, cell encapsulation (cell covering), and immobilisation of structures that hold up cells. It is also based on advances in the understanding of the features that control cell behaviour and wound healing, such as matrix of materials outside cells, growth factors and the immune system. Since tissue engineering involves the redoing of the steps involved in embryological development, this field can be considered a form of applied developmental biology (UofT, p.1).

The bioartificial kidney will be made in the same way that an artificial pancreas or liver would be made. Insulin producing cells or liver cells are microencapsulated to a polymeric membrane and transplanted as replacement organs. Because the cells are encapsulated, the host does not require anti-rejection drugs (UofT p.2). There are a number of other uses for tissue engineering, but here we are mainly interested in the bioartificial kidney.

The kidney was the first organ to be transplanted and also the first organ to have a machine made to replace its function, namely the dialysis machine. It looks like the kidney will be the first solid organ to be replaced by tissue engineering.

David Humes of the University of Michigan has already created an outside the body renal assistance device for patients suffering from acute renal failure. It runs blood through a device outside the body attached to the person in order to speed recovery. This device is hoped to be a step toward the final goal which is an implantable replacement for kidneys in chronic renal failure. This device may at first extend the time between dialysis treatments for patients in chronic renal failure and they hope to create an erythropoietin-secreting device to combat the low hemoglobin of kidney patients. These endeavours are being undertaken by a private laboratory. A bioartificial kidney is still some way away, but intermediate like the renal assistance device are hoped to be deployed sooner (Humes, 1999).

Besides secreting hormones, the kidneys cleanse the blood in two ways. First, the blood is grossly filtered by driving it through structure consisting of a wall of tangled capillaries called the glomerulus. Under increased pressure, small molecules are driven through the capillaries' leaky walls. A great deal of water and other valuable small molecules are also filtered out in the process. All of this ultrafiltrate is captured and funnelled through a looping tube, whose walls are made of specialized cells. These cells have evolved to recapture the water and the "good" molecules and return them to general circulation, while leaving the waste to drain away to the bladder and be voided from the body(Humes, 1998, p.1).

As we can see, filtration is a two step process consisting of gross filtration followed by selective resorption. Dialysis as it is, now only reproduces step one, the gross filtration. The artificial kidney now used in dialysis is comprised of thousands of fine hollow fibers with permeable walls. The patient's blood laden with metabolic wastes is diverted through the fibers. These are bathed in a fluid that draws off waste molecules. This lifesaving treatment still leaves people with serious health problems (Humes, 1998, p.1).

The approach taken by David Humes's laboratory is to recreate the kidney's two step filtration with an artificial two step process. They are developing a filter to be linked in series with a reabsorbing unit. If both steps can be made efficient, the path will be clear to creating an implantable device (ibid. p.2).

A recent discovery in the laboratory of David Humes increased the feasibility of making a bioartificial kidney. Among the reabsorbing cells that comprise the wall of the reabsorbing tubule (Loop of Henly), are certain stem cells that retain a fetal-like capability of rapidly expanding and developing into specialized cells. David Humes's laboratory has created techniques for collecting these cells and expanding their numbers outside the body, making them available for incorporation into an absorbing device to replace the Loop of Henle (Humes, 1998, p,2),

The reabsorbing device begins with a porous hollow fiber, such as that used in the standard artificial kidney in a dialysis machine. The inner surface of this fiber is lined with living tubule cells, which are first precoated with a matrix to support cell growth. The cells arrange themselves in a natural array, forming a functioning tubule. Experiments have proven that the cells do function, reabsorbing filtrate at clinically useful rates (Humes, 1998, p.2).

This discussion has so far addressed mostly the kidney's role in eliminating toxic waste. Now we will discuss some other important functions of the kidney. The kidney, among other things is the body's chief regulator of red blood cells. Certain cells in the kidney sense the level of oxygen being delivered to the tissues. In response, these kidney cells produce and secrete erythropoietin (EPO). This stimulates bone marrow to produce red blood cells. The kidney cells stop producing EPO when they sense adequate oxygenation of the tissues. This is a feedback loop in which one situation affects another and the other situation corrects the original situation. The goal is to create a steady state called homeostasis.

An individual in kidney failure loses the ability to monitor and adjust tissue oxygenation through red blood cell production. Red blood cells contain hemoglobin, containing iron which transports oxygen in the body. People in kidney failure, lacking EPO often become severely anemic and sometimes need blood transfusions. EPO injections help but they are not as good as a real kidney's feedback loop. Dr. Humes's lab is working on a way to include EPO making cells as part of the bioartificial kidney (Humes, 1998, p.3).

Even without a perfect bioartificial kidney, an implantable filter along would increase the length of time between dialysis sessions. Other critical functions of the kidney such as regulating blood pressure, producing renin and angiotensin, maintaining calcium balance through calcitriol, maintaining sodium balance, and maintaining integrity of the immune system are hoped to be incorporated into the bioartificial kidney through the emerging discipline of tissue engineering. Tissue engineering is an exciting part of biomedical engineering (ibid, p.3).

My original goal was to extrapolate from a natural kidney and a dialysis machine. When I looked at the nephron, the functional unit of the kidney, and the dialysis machine, I concluded that a bioartificial kidney was impossible. This idea was further strengthened by reading. Dr. Edward Cole further confirmed my pessissm about bioartificial kidneys. As a last try, I called Dr. Michael Sefton, head of biomedical engineering at University of Toronto, who told me that it was indeed feasible to make an implantable artificial kidney and that scientists at the University of Michigan were working on it. When I looked up the bioartificial kidney at University of Toronto science library, I found six articles by Dr. John Woods and Dr. David Humes about their work on bioartificial kidneys. Their work was more brilliant than I could imagine, and now I feel optimistic that a bioartificial kidney will be made one day. There is a saying that new problems can only be solved by new ideas (Combden, 1998).

Obstacles To Making A Bioartificial Kidney

1. It is unclear whether proximal tubule progenitor cells are able to differentiate into other kidney segment cells. The early indication is that they can (a) because they recover after acute injury and (b) because recovery can be made after acute tubular necrosis. Growth factors, TGF-B1 (tubular growth factor) and ECF (extracellular growth factor) along with retinoid

and retinoic acid, promoted tubulogenesis in renal tubule progenitor cells in tissue culture. This finding is one of the first definitions of inductive factors which may be important in making a mammalian organ (Humes and Cieslinski, 1993,pp 678-698).

2.	There needs to be considerable pressure to move the water and solutes from one part of a semipermeable membrane to another. The approach taken by Dr. Humes is to use heat and an electric charge called convection to move particles from one end to another. Convective transport has been achieved outside living cells with the use of polysulphone hollow fibers.

3.	Bleeding associated with required anticoagulation is a problem. In order to solve this problem, endothelial cell seeding of small calibre vascular prostheses have been shown to reduce clotting. With regard to preventing clots, another avenue is open. Transferring genes into endothelial cells for the production of an anticoagulant protein that will work locally so that no bleeding is caused is clearly conceivable as a solution (Humes, 1993, pp. 2033).

4.	The above ideas can replace the need for anticoagulants as well as preventing clots, which is the fourth obstacle to producing a bioartificial kidney (Humes, 1993, pp.678-679).

5.	The fifth obstacle to producing a bioartificial kidney is rejection of foreign tissue. One of the solutions to this problem is to grow the biomaterials from the patient's own cells. Also, encapsulating foreign cells so that they do not contact cells of the body, such as circulating blood can eliminate the problem of rejection (Cutler, 1998).

6.	A sixth obstacle to producing an effective bioartificial kidney is diminution of filtration rate due to protein deposition or clotting, or both. This has been solved by using endothelial (inside the body) seeded conduits along the filtration devices. Cells from the patient's body (usually blood vessel cells) are used to eliminate the problem of rejection of foreign tissue.

RELAXATION

A person's courage is dependent on his willingness to have it divided by his inability to relax. Besides, relaxation decreases anxiety and feels good and improves health. For a quick relaxation routine try running the following through your mind. Start from the outside and work inward. Sit back comfortably in the chair, let your skin get looser, looser, looser... Let your muscles go completely limp. Let your joints get further and further apart. Let your bones get softer, softer, softer...Let your heart go soft and your blood vessels dilate. Generate a tingling in your hands and feet. Slow down a nerve message from your head to your toes from 120 feet per second to 119.9 feet per second. Let your internal organs relax. Let your arms get heavier and warmer. Let your legs get heavier and warmer. Now be supremely calm.

When we are anxious or depressed there are three things going on. First is irrational, catastrophic thoughts. Second is muscle tension and third is that our senses stop admitting information to our brains. By combatting these three things, we can dwell in the here and now and rid anxiety and depression.

2.   In the chair or bed, slow down your breathing from 16-20 breaths per minute to 3-6 breaths per minute. This makes a more relaxing chemistry of the blood by making it more alkaline. Then, muscle relaxation. Tense and relax forehead by wrinking it for 10 seconds, then relax 30 seconds. Then, neck, chest, abdomen, back, arms, legs, hips, feet and hands in the same way. Take a slow, deep breath.

3.   Dwell in the present, not the future or past. Become aware of sights (beauty), sounds, touch, kinesthetic (awareness of limb position), smells, and taste. Let them all be a comfort to you.

4.   Find irrational, catastrophic thoughts. Let them float out of your body as good thoughts like vacations float in. Remember that what we worry about usually never comes to pass.

5.   Visualize good things happening and pleasant scenes.

6.   Self-hypnosis. Stare at your thumbs, relax completely and get ready to count from three to one. At one you will be asleep in a focused trance. Give yourself the suggestion that every time you take a slow, deep breath, you will relax. Count from zero to three and come out of the trance feeling good.

Jacobson's Progressive Muscle Relaxation

Do each tensing contraction for ten seconds, then relax for half a minute to a minute.

1.   Wrinkle your forehead.

2.   Close the eyelids tightly.

3.   Lift up the muscles on the sides of the nose.

4.   Purse lips.

5.   Tighten jaws, clench teeth.

6.   Tense neck.

7.   Shrug shoulders.

8.   Tense arms.

9.   Hold a deep breath. Feel tension in chest, abdomen and back.

10.   Tense legs.

Autogenics

Autogenic training consists of giving yourself suggestions about your body like:

1. My arms and legs are heavy
2. My arms and legs are warm.
3. My chest feels calm and pleasant
4. My stomach is soft and warm.
5. My heartbeat is calm and steady.
6. My forehead is cool.
7. My breathing is calm and slow, ever slowing.
8. I am supremely calm.

Go over your body with these suggestions and let your muscles go soft and completely limp. An ability to bring relaxation over yourself quickly helps you to meet adversity.

Sensory Awareness

Becoming aware of the information coming in from all five senses helps you relax. Also, becoming detached from your environment, making your eyes like a movie camera and your ears like a tape recorder helps you relax. Doing anything that gives you pleasure helps you relax as well. Enjoying your work helps you relax. Another technique that is often helpful is conscious thought control, as well as you can do. Say that you will be calm and cheerful all day long. Psycho-imagination therapy consists of fantasizing what you want, then taking action. All these help control your thoughts and stay calm.

Relaxation Routines

To start with, think about your body. The shape of your skin and the position of your body and notice all the points of contact between your body and the chair. Notice also where you are touching yourself. If your hands are not already on your tummy, move them there.

Now I want you to start doing two things at once. The first is to keep noticing all the points of contact between your body and the chair, and the second thing is to notice how your body moves, indeed how you move your body as you breathe in and as you breathe out...very gradually... I want you to exaggerate the movement as you breathe in... exaggerate by getting more air into your lungs and allowing your ribcage to expand...as you breathe out exaggerate the motion by taking as much time as you can to exhale. I want you to use my silence as an opportunity to carry out the exercise that I set before I keep quiet. So right now...spend maybe a minute breathing in deeply, filling your lungs with air, expanding your ribcage as you breathe in and then taking as much time as you can to breathe out. Check quickly now, to make sure that you are still noticing all the points of contact between your body and the chair. Notice also where you are touching yourself. The pressure of your hands on your body and notice how, as you breathe in and out, you move your hands up and down. Notice also any other movements that you make. Now, I want you to start seriously focusing on relaxing your body, starting with the surface of your skin and gradually moving deeper and deeper inside your body, so that eventually you have control of all your internal organs, the autonomic nervous system and brain function.

Now, starting with your skin...when you are ready... as you breathe out, allow your skin to soften and relax. All you have to do is imagine that your skin becomes loose and hangs loose from your body. I think you will find this easier to accomplish if you start imagining your body becomes loose as you breathe out. Use the time that you spend breathing in to prepare yourself to let your skin relax as you breathe out. So that the more you practice the more you prepare yourself for the rest of your life to let your skin relax as you breathe out. And every now and again, without any instructions, make sure that you are still aware of the points of contact between your body and the chair... aware of the places where you are touching yourself, always conscious of the way you move your body as you breathe out and breathe in. And about now, if you wish to, notice the state of your muscles. The next time you breathe out, in addition to letting your skin loosen on your body, let your muscles relax, soften, go limp, so that after a little while you are using absolutely no energy.

Just allow your body to sink deeply into the chair. Maintain your slow, rhythmic breathing...filling your lungs with air and expanding your ribcage as you breathe in... taking as much time as you can to breathe out. Now, if you wish to, as you finish exhaling, wait for two or three seconds as you breathe in again. Notice the experience of neither breathing in or breathing out. Let your breathing apparatus grind to a complete halt for two or three seconds. Use that time to let your skin and muscles relax even more. Allow yourself to relax so deeply that you become aware only of your intention to relax and the sound of my voice. If, while you are relaxing something should happen, a sound, the telephone ringing, a knock on the door, ignore these sounds. Check quickly to make sure that you are still in touch with the chair, noticing all the points of contact between your body and the chair. Notice again where you are touching yourself. Notice your slow, rhythmic breathing. Make sure you breathe as deeply as you want to, that you spend as much time breathing out as you want to. Check to see if you are pausing for a second or two, or three, before you breathe in.

Now, start thinking about the bones in your body. Part of the truths about human bodies is that we all have more cells in our brain than we have in our body. The cells in our brain control the cells in our body and if you choose to you can use your brain to allow your bones to soften. They might not soften much, but they will soften measurably, just as if you choose to, and I am asking you not to choose to, you could harden the bones in your body. Instead, I am asking you to soften them. Notice how you move your body as you breathe in and out, but in a moment as you breathe out, concentrate all your effort on allowing your bones to relax and soften and feel a little rubbery or jelly-like.

If your imagination is good, pretend that you are seven weeks old, lying in the crib and your bones soft, rubbery and flexible, jelly-like, breathing comfortably, trusting the crib...to take the full weight of your body...just as you now trust the chair to take the full weight of your body. Each time you begin to breathe out you allow your skin and your muscles and your bones to relax a little more.

Now, I am interrupting what you are doing, because I want you to think about all the joints in your body. Just as you have 200 or so bones, you have 200 or so joints. Without thinking about any particular joint, but instead about all of them, allow the joints in your body to loosen, but as you do that get your shoulder blades a little closer together behind your back. Use a little effort to stretch your neck and hold your head up...a little effort to move the points of your shoulders away from your ears and use a little energy to move every joint a little. Give your body a workout. Make sure that you can wiggle your toes and the joints of your toes. Check the joints in your ankles, your knees...the joints in your finger...thumbs, hands wrists...elbows...shoulders. Think of the joints between your vertebrae. Move your spinal column, a little like a snake, to make sue that the the joint is moved...right...left...centre...up and down. Having done that, check again to make sure that your body is in good contact with the chair, that your breathing is still slow and rhythmic. Every time you breathe out, your skin relaxes a little, your muscles relax a little, your bones soften a little, your joints loosen a little, so that now you are in a position to think about your heart beating and the gentle flow of the blood through your blood vessels. I want you to use your brain and deliberately soften your muscles more, so that your blood vessels can expand and thus make it easier for your heart to pump blood through your circulatory system. Indeed, the more you allow your skin and muscles to relax, the slower your heart needs to beat, the less pressure there is in the blood circulation. You will save yourself energy that you can use for other things. And, if as you allow your muscles to relax, so that your blood vessels really do expand and you find blood reaching the tips of your capillaries near the surface of your skin. Do not be surprised if you get a tingling feeling in your legs or your hands, or your face, or your forehead.

Indeed, the thing to do right now is to see if you can actually generate a tingling feeling, or signals that the blood is filling your capillaries right to the tip near the surface of your skin. And, as you find that you can generate a tingling feeling, so allow your skin to relax more and muscles, your bones, and your joints to relax more. See if you can get a sense, or feel of blood circulating throughout your body. Maybe you can feel the pulse in your tummy, or a sense of a very strong pulse in your neck, or perhaps you can feel a pulse in your hands when your hands are touching. If you can get in touch with your pulse and you slow, rhythmic breathing, so you are in touch with two vital signs of life.... respiration and pulse. So you are in touch with your own aliveness. When you can do that you are ready to get in touch with your nervous system itself... ready to use your brain to control the rest of your nervous system.

I want you to use your ears and start noticing the traffic sounds and I want you to use every traffic sound as a source of comfort, so that your body instead of being start by sound, relaxes to the sound. I want you to allow your nervous system to slow down. Let the sounds comfort you.

Ordinarily, I am told, your nervous system can pass a message through your body through a particular nerve at the rate of about 120 feet per second.

So very quickly now, settle back into your chair. Notice all the points of contact between your body and the chair... Notice how you move your body as you breathe in and out. Relax your skin, your muscles, your bones, and your joints. It should generate a tingling feeling in your hands to the tips of your fingers. You will get a warm feeling in your cheeks... as the warm blood circulating through your body reaches the surface of your skin. Let your toes, feet, heels and ankles go absolutely limp. Tighten the muscles in your legs so that your feet begin to tingle as warm blood reaches the very tips of your toes. Touch your ears to notice sounds coming from other parts of the house..... sounds inside the room...sounds of traffic. Allow the sounds to be a source of comfort and use your brain to slow down the rest of your nervous system, so that instead of being startled by the sounds, no matter how loud, your body relaxes as your eardrums become aware of the vibrating air, and let the messages that pass through your nervous system slow down from what might be 120 feet per second to 119.9 feet per second. Use your brain to conserve nervous energy. Use the energy that you save to enable you to think clearly... to think concisely. Use the energy that you save to help you recall things that you have read, to concentrate on what you are reading. Use the energy that you save to help you memorize things that need to be learned. And from time to time check to make sure that your skin and your muscles and your bones and your joints are indeed relaxing a little each time you breathe out. Use your brain so that you become in control of your body, instead of your body controlling you. Make sure that your body is acting and reacting the way you want it to, instead of acting and reacting involuntarily.

So, once again and quickly, deliberately relax your skin, deliberately relax your muscles, deliberately allow your bones to soften. Deliberately allow your joints to loosen a little. Do not be surprised if while you are practicing your relaxation exercises your body twitches or jerks. Do not be surprised if you experience a tingling feeling in some parts of your body. All of these are good signs that your body is relaxing.

See if you can get in touch with your heart beat by sensing a pulse somewhere in your body. Of course if you can barely notice a pulse, at the same time you are aware of your slow, rhythmic breathing, then you are in touch with your aliveness. Two important vital signs of life. When you are in touch with your pulse and your heartbeat you are ready to relax all of your internal organs, without knowing the specific names or specific locations of any. You can use your brain to relax your abdomen and everything inside it. You can use your brain to untie any knots in your stomach.

So, with your body relaxed, you hear more keenly, you see more clearly. Your taste improves. Your sense of smell is heightened. With your body relaxed and your mind clear, your jogging becomes more valuable. You will discover that you can jog with less effort, but as you jog, each time you breathe out, relax your body a little. Allow the blood to circulate through your blood vessels more freely as you jog. Use your lungs more efficiently to extract oxygen from the air. Improve your metabolism. Vitalize your brain cells by providing them with an ample supply of oxygen. Use the nervous energy that you save to improve your memory, your power of concentration. Use your brain so that as you study you relax. Make your memorizing a relaxing procedure instead of a stressful one. Use your brain to train your memory to function in a relaxed way to store information with ease. For all I know, this might require that you read more slowly and remember more efficiently, reading only once with improved recall, improved recognition, and flashback for what you have read. It is the ability to turn on a flashback that is important.

So very quickly notice all the points of contact between your body and the chair. Notice how you move your body as you breathe in and out. Once again and quickly, as you breathe out, let your skin and muscles and bones and joints go limp and soft.... relax. Make sure your brain is clear. That you listen to sounds, noticin the small amount of light that comes in through your closed eyelids. Make sure you notice the draft in your nostrils as you breathe in and out. Explore the inside of your mouth with your tongue. Search for taste sensations. And be ready in a little while to open your eyes and look around the room. But first, when you are ready, take two enormously deep breaths. Fill your lungs to almost bursting. Do not hold your breath. Breathe out slowly, noisily if necessary. Continue to relax as you breathe out. Prepare yourself so that as you finish breathing out the second time you are ready to open your eyes. Look around the room, elevate your body,then reach out and turn off the tape recorder.

ANTICANCER

1. Avoid smoke and pollution.

2. Stay lean. Keep your body mass index between 20 and 25. Avoid carbonated drinks and decrease energy-dense food. Avoid sugar and fat.

3. Limit meat consumption.

4. Eat two thirds of a meal fruits, nuts and legumes and whole grains.

5. Move and exercise.

6. Decrease alcohol consumption.

7. Decrease salt consumption.

8. Decrease sun exposure. Wear a hat, clothing and sunblock.

9. Avoid promiscuous sex and vaccinate against human papilloma virus, hepatitis B and C.

The main risk factors for disease according to the world health organization in order of importance are:

1. smoking 2. high body fat percentage. 3. high blood pressure. 4. high blood sugar. 5. inactivity. 6. insufficient fruits 7. alcohol. 8. insufficient nuts and seeds. 9. high cholesterol. 10. illegal drugs. 11. excess salt. 12. processed meats. 13. insufficient vegetables 14. air pollution. And 15. trans fat.

BLOOD VESSELS

Following the heart healthy suggestions in this book will keep your blood vessels healthy and disease-free.

Throwing Everything We Know At Heart Disease, Naturally

Heart disease is the leading cause of death in North America. This is a short essay that is a prelude to a book that is being written in point form. A more comprehensive book form will be released when I get time to write it.

1. Prioritize exercise – do whatever you are able

2. Have a good family life and loving partner.

3. Eat primarily vegetarian and a rainbow of foods.

4. Avoid sugar

5. Avoid salt.

6. Get enough sleep.

7. Do relaxation

8. Schedule time for others and yourself.

9. Optimize medication and supplements.

10. Have a healthy sex life.

11. Be relaxed and laid back as much as possible.

12. Keep an optimal weight.

13. Stop eating when 80 % full.

14. Take clopidogrel.

15. Take a daily 81 mg. Aspirin

16. Avoid smoke and second-hand smoke.

17. Avoid anger and hostility.

18. Look for opportunities to move.

19. Have enjoyable leisure time activities.

20. Avoid too much protein.

21. Have regular checkups and follow doctor's advice.

22. Avoid overwork.

23. Never retire and engage in satisfying work.

24. Avoid poverty, poor nutrition, and air pollution.

25. Maintain good mental health – avoid distress.

26. Avoid cortisone, anabolic steroids, immune suppressants and excess vitamins AorD.

27. Eat oatmeal, almonds, flaxseeds, beans, metamucil, apples, margarine with phytosterols, soy protein and garlic.

28. Walk 10-30 minutes daily.

29. Care for teeth and hygiene.

30. Practice kindness.

31. Maintain good posture.

32. Drink 8-12 cups water daily.

33. Avoid fatigue.

34. Have fun.

35. Don't sweat the small stuff.

36. Get a stress-free pet.

37. Stretch

38. Diversify exercise – make interesting.

39. Stay positive with good and bad days.

40. Keep saturated fat less than 7% of daily calories.

41. No trans, hydrogenated or partially hydrogenated fats.

42. No fried foods – no French fries, doughnuts, cookies, or crackers

43. monounsaturated and polyunsaturated fats.

44. Eat oily fish eg. Salmon, tuna, mackerel, or herring

45. 1g omega-3 fatty acid supplement per day.

46. Eat a handful of peanuts, walnuts, or almonds per day.

47. Use canola, olive, peanut or safflower oil instead of vegetable oil.

48. Eat avocados.

49. No ice-cream, fats, frozen desserts, or cholesterol.

50. Use lean cuts of meat.

51. Use chicken breasts or drumsticks instead of wings or thighs.

52. Whole-grain cereals.

53. Eat out only once per week.

54. Avoid liquid calories and colas.

55. Reduce portions.

56. Avoid supersizing items.

57. Avoid all you can eat buffets.

58. No mayo, cheese, fries or shakes.

59. Avoid appetizers.

60. No skin on chicken.

61. Avoid rich sauces and cream.

62. Use herbs and spices in lieu of salt or butter.

63. Eat soy or tofu.

64. Eat fresh fruit.

65. Limit simple sugars and carbohydrates.

66. Alcohol in moderation.

67. No second helpings.

68. Use garlic.

69. Eat fibre – apples, figs, beets, Brussels sprouts, yams, beans, chick peas, pinto beans, brown rice, and bran flakes.

70. Consider statins.

71. Take niacin.

72. Take lycopene and Co Q 10.

73. Eat sardines.

74. Floss and brush regularly.

75. No worry about money.

76. Hugs 4x per day or more.

77. Relax each day.

78. No anxiety.

79. No irritability or anger.

80. Feel optimistic.

81. Learn constantly.

82. Enjoy life.

83. Feel that you are as good as other people.

84. Enjoy life.

85. Use green and black tea.

86. Lift weights.

87. Use cocoa, broccoli, and chocolate.

88. Avoid excess heat and cold.

89. Take in sunshine and vitamin D.

90. Avoid pollution and noise.

91. Know your C-reactive protein.

92. Take astaxanthin, Krill oil, policosanol, and sytrinol

93.   Take arginine.

94.   Eat carrots, onions, and mushrooms.

95.   Eat kiwi, mangoes, pineapple, and fruit salad.

96.   Eat chile peppers and popcorn.

97.   Eat artichokes.

98.   Drink tea, grape juice, milk.

99.   Take calcium.

100. Take chromium

101. Take saponins eg Cholestaid, alfalfa.

102. Use guggul and hawthorn.

103. Eat 4 or more meals per day (small).

104. Take fenugreek.

105. Take ginger and ginger pills.

106. Use dandelions and bitters.

107. Give blood.

108. Eat calories early in the day.

109. Carry uncoated aspirin with you.

110. massage

111. accupressure

112. aloe.

113. phenylalanine, tryptophan, methionine, lysine, leucine, isoleucine, valine, histidine, and threoning, essential amino acids.

114. l-carnitine

115. alpha lipoic acid.

116. pycnogenol and turmeric.

117. milk thistle and astragalus.

118. Thiamine, vitamin Briboflavin, BB6.

119. bromelain and papain.

120. cryptoxanthin and zeaxanthaxin.

121. lutein.

122. chamomile.

123. cayenne.

124. conjugated linlenic acid.

125. chitosan before each meal.

126. hydroxycitric acid.

127. feverfew

128. gelsenium

129. licorice.

130. imagine pleasant scenes.

131. passionflower.

132. prayer.

133. quercetin.

134. selenium

135. vitamins C,D, and E.

136. magnesium

137. N-acetylcysteine.

138. copper and curry.

139. chlorophyll and celery, parsley and cucumber.

140. juicing

141. blueberries and hibiscus flower extract.

142. natto.

143. manuka honey.

144. oat bran and cod liver oil.

145. deep breathing.

146. fresh dandelion wine from health food shop.

147. eat lightly and be aware of what you are eating.

148. bee pollen, barley grass, wild cherry bark, capsicum, red clover. Chlorophyll, pau d'Arco.

149. burdock root, alfalfa, red clover, sea greens, yellow dock root, burberry bark

150. glucomannans.

151. plantain and cinammon.

152. grapeseed extract.

153. pine bark.

154. l-arginine and l-citrulline.

155. glutathione, melatonin and curcumin and resveratrol.

156. sesame seeds, Wakame seaweed and whey protein

157. limit caffeine.

158. d-ribose

159. R-lipoic acid and vitamin K.

160. dimethyl glycine

161. Vanadium and biotin

162. glucosamine and MSM.

163. chelated molybdenum

164. Captomer and dimercaptosuccinic acid

165. egg whites.

166. pectin.

EXERCISE

Exercise is essential to health and character. As a nurse, I learned that we must do all that we can to move, although that varies greatly depending on health and circumstances. The theme of this book is playing your cards to the utmost.

Benefits of Exercise

1. Increases your self-confidence and self-esteem.

2. Improves your digestion.

3. Helps you sleep better.

4. Gives you more energy.

5. Makes you look healthy.

6. Strengthens your immune system.

7. Improves your body shape.

8. Burns up extra calories.

9. Tones and trims your muscles.

10. Promotes muscle definition.

11. Improves circulation and helps lower blood pressure.

12. Lifts your spirits.

13. Reduces tension and stress.

14. Helps you to lose weight and maintain it.

15. Makes you limber and flexible.

16. Builds strength.

17. Improves endurance.

18. Increases lean muscle.

19. Increases appetite and better food choices.

20. Alleviates menstrual cramps.

21. Improves muscle and nerve chemistry.

22. Increases metabolism.

23. Improves coordination and balance.

24. Improves posture.

25. Rids back problems and pain.

26. Uses calories better.

27. Lowers resting heart rate and strengthens heart.

28. Increases muscle size.

29. Improves glycogen and energy storage.

30. Causes better nutrient use.

31. Increases fat-burning enzymes.

32. Increases number and size of mitochondria in muscles and heart.

33. Strengthens bones.

34. Enhances oxygen transport.

35. Increases myoglobin, therefore oxygen use by muscles.

36. Improves liver function.

37. Increases muscle speed and reaction time.

38. Enhances nervous system communication.

39. Strengthens heart.

40. Improves blood flow.

41. Eases varicose veins by increasing venous tone.

42. Improves stroke volume of heart which improves exercise tolerance.

43. Increases contractility of heart's ventricles which pump blood improving stroke volume.

44. Increases heart size and weight.

45. Increases contractility of heart.

46. Improves calcium transport in heart and muscles making them work better.

47. Helps prevent heart disease and cancer.

48. Increases HDL "good" cholesterol which cleans arteries.

49. Decreases bad LDL cholesterol which clogs arteries.

50. Decreases cholesterol.

51. Decreases triglycerides.

52. Increases hemoglobin in red blood cells, improving oxygenation.

53. Decreases blood acids.

54. Improves lactic acid uptake, therefore improves exercise tolerance.

55. Improves heart rate recovery after exercise.

56. Improves capillary opening during exercise.

57. Improves blood flow to muscles.

58. Enhances cardiovascular and cardiorespiratory function.

59. Improves alveolar function for breathing.

60. Increases CO_2 tolerance.

61. Improves O_2 uptake.

62. Improves bone metabolism.

63. Improves bone density decreasing osteoporosis.

64. Improves development and strength of connective tissue.

65. Increases recovery from illness and injury.

66. Enhances neuromuscular and general relaxation.

67. Alleviates depression and anxiety.

68. Improves emotional stability.

69. Enhances mental clarity.

70. Causes good feeling.

71. Improves sweating, therefore heat adaptation.

72. Enhances cold adaptation.

73. Improves body composition.

74. Decreases fat tissue.

75. Improves agility.

76. Increases positivity about life.

77. Increases epinephrine that improves mood as well as serotonin for same.

78. Stimulates pain killing endorphins.

79. Alleviates constipation.

80. Improves adrenalin use meaning more energy and less stress.

81. Helps you tolerate stress.

82. Enables you to meet new friends and develop fulfilling relationships.

83. Helps you move past self-imposed limitations.

84. Improves zest and appreciation for life with increased self-respect.

85. Improves physical activity enjoyment.

86. Positive addiction to exercise improves negative addictions.

87. Gives you a greater desire to participate in life – to take more risks because of increased self-confidence and self-esteem.

88. Improves sports performance.

89. Improves quality of life.

90. Improves sex life, romance and marriage.

91. Increases life span, perhaps an extra hour of life for every hour of exercise.

92. Makes you feel control or mastery over your life and the belief that you can create any reality you want.

93. Self-control, spontaneity, and independence is improved.

94. Improves whole body function.

95. Reduces joint discomfort.

96. Increases range of motion.

97. Stimulates and improves concentration.

98. Increases tolerance of all people, broadens outlook, and helps tolerance of athletes.

99. If done enough decreases appetite.

100. Decreases irritability.

101. Causes feeling of well-being and accomplishment.

102. Invigorates body and mind.

103. Helps enjoyment of nature and outdoors.

104. Increases body awareness.

105. Reduces or prevents boredom.

106. Improves gait.

107. Improves whole brain thinking.

108. Relaxes brain.

109. Improves problem-solving sometimes effortless.

110. Gives a clearer perspective on ideas, issues, problems and challenges.

111. Releases blockages and limitations in thinking.

112. Helps you be someone of achievement.

113. Helps you realize your fullest potential.

114. Reduces illness and improves life span.

115. Improves well-being and appearance.

116. Makes you feel more alive in your spirit.

117. Greatly improves outlook for mental illness and major mental illness.

118. Greatly improves self-control and will power, improving all types of courage and good behaviour. Diana Nyad is an extreme example of using will power to control fear and pain.

119. Physical courage is not likely if your body is unwilling. Also improves morale which also improves physical, moral and personal courage.

120. Helps you toughen to handle life's challenges and hard knocks with grace.

LOGOTHERAPY AND MENTAL HEALTH

The basic principle logotherapy is finding meaning in life. If someone has a why, he can withstand any how, including torture and death.

Logotherapy was invented by Victor Frankl, a holocaust survivor. He gives two techniques associated with it. One is paradoxical intention. It involves trying to make the feeling as bad as you can make it and you will find that it cannot be made bad. This often takes away the fear of the feeling and the problem goes away.

The other technique is dereflection. It involves not focussing on the problem and maybe it will not bother you so much.

The decision as to which therapy to use depends on the nature of the problem. Each one can be tried to see if it works.

One needs meaning and a sense of responsibility to his existence, which is a form of existential analysis. To live is to suffer, to survive is to find meaning in life. Examples are a good conscience and helping people. Everyone is unique, which means that his meaning is unique. For Jack Lalanne it was to improve people's health and well-being by setting an example.

Meaning can be achieved by doing a deed, by experiencing a value, or by suffering, to name a few.

Experiencing can involve experiencing something such as a work of nature or culture or someone such as a love. Part of love is to grasp another person in the innermost core of his or her personality. For suffering to have meaning, it must be necessary, otherwise it is masochism, not heroism. Suffering gives life more meaning than a life of wealth and ease. Suffering purifies sin. Our purpose makes "an immortal footprint in the sands of time." An optimist files away in his torn away wall calendar, desires. These can be work done and love loved and suffering bravely suffered – sometimes the things of which we are most proud. This helps us to deal with our fear of death. Suffering and meaning are often for God's sake.

Logotherapy shows one how to transform pain, death, and guilt into triumph, by showing a sense of responsibility, bravery, and tolerance of suffering.

One's life should be directed toward something "other" or greater than oneself.

Conscience can be creative and can mold itself to the situation such as survival, and the fact that a man is not held accountable when he is under duress or did not know at the time, as in psychosis.

Cognitive-Behavioural Therapy

The steps in CBT are:

1. If you have enough insight, learn how the problem develops and perpetuates.

2. Spot self-critical thoughts.

3. Combat them – suggest alternative beliefs.

4. Enhance self-acceptance, make a list of your qualities, talents, skills and strengths.

5. Give yourself credit for what you do and did.

6. Daily Activity Diary (DAD) note what you did, and record pleasure and mastery.

7. Write down self-critical thoughts and suggest alternatives e.g. I'm never going to finish this. This is not worth doing. So I did this? So what? I haven't done enough.

8. Introduce changes. Plan ahead.

9.   Change rules for living and Bottom Line.

10. Pick out pre-occupations and themes.

11. Criticizing others criticizes yourself and vice versa.

12. Suggest alternative rules.

13. Undermine the Bottom Line. What evidence supports the new Bottom Line and undermines the old one. For example (1) observations. (2) behavioural experiments.

14. Create an action plan eg goals.

15. Create a list of activities that support good feelings and goals.

16. Let higher self-esteem improve relationships and behaviour and thinking.

HEART AND SPIRIT

If you follow the suggestions in this book, you will develop your heart and spirit.

How To Develop Courage and Self-Respect

What I Have Found Works

As a psychotherapist specializing in overcoming fear and anxiety, I am not only an academic expert on courage, but overcoming fear and adversity have been the story of my life and I and some others feel that I have done it very well. I will show this in the following pages and tell the underlying methods that I used.

The first major difficulty that I encountered in life was agoraphobia due to the distorted perceptions of schizotypal disorder. I overcame it very well, with little help from doctors or family members, except perhaps my parents who insisted that I do more and more. I got over it by doing more and more in the open spaces, leading canoe trips, and physical activity.

By age fifteen, I had overcome it completely and played varsity football, also excelling at academics, which previously I had not been keen on. A cruel psychiatrist was upset at how well I was doing and assaulted me very brutally causing the toughest and longest fight of my whole life, my battle with paranoid schizophrenia. It has caused a hellish, nightmarish suffering for most of 49 years and counting. The odd time it caused others to suffer as well. Schizophrenia is the most serious mental disease you can get and arguably the most serious disease known to man. It is life-threatening and reduces your lifespan by thirty years. This shows that I have struggled with adversity and made the most of it. I accomplished a great deal, but would have accomplished much more without schizophrenia

What Courage Is and Why It Matters

Courage is basically the ability to control yourself and your behaviour in fear, pain, danger, death, or adversity. It is basically a matter of using will power to do this. Will power is dependent primarily on how much you want to do something. Will power is want power. Courage is dependent on how much you want to have it.

One important thing to know is that we must not hurt or risk ourselves at any time to show courage. Courage is something everyone has and you cannot live without it. Having good mental health enables us to use willpower effectively, so that although my battle with schizophrenia shows courage, schizophrenia saps my functional courage and diminishes my production greatly. Schizophrenia causes a constant desire to do bad things so that refraining from these and living a constructive life is a sign of courage. This is also true for anyone.

Courage correlates with conscience and morality. My ability to take a punch, including bareknuckle, is caused by conscience, as is my ability to take pain. The righteous gentiles' behaviour in sheltering us from the Nazis was caused by conscience. Conscience and self-control are intimately intertwined and constantly increase from birth to death. If conscience and self-control were a sign of immaturity, as some of my family members think, it would decrease from birth to death, which does not occur.

Courage is the ultimate virtue. It stops all that is bad for us to do and causes all that is good. We live today because of humanity's courage. The difference between an altruist and a hero is one of degree, with an altruist showing some courage and a hero showing more.

With regard to self-control, self-discipline is a form of it, usually applied day-to-day on a long term basis. Athletic training, work and study are forms of self-discipline as is writing.

Since a sense of responsibility comes from maturity, courage is related to responsibility. An example would be a man who took full responsibility for patients being late for therapy at Grace Hospital. He got chewed out, but didn't mind. That took courage. I also appreciated what he did because it saved the rest of us.

Thrill-seeking, as in certain daredevil activities, is the opposite of self-discipline and roughly opposite to courage.

There are many different types of courage. Ones that come to mind, most noteably are physical courage, as in facing danger or pain, moral courage as in doing the right thing, personal courage as in overcoming personal demons, and psychological courage as in enduring psychic pain for benefit, such as enduring fear to get over a phobia. Bill Clinton's facing criticism for not serving in the military is an example of moral courage in order to show principle. The same with Muhammad Ali.

Psychological courage is also overcoming a fear of losing the mind as in dealing with a psychosis. Another example is someone who overcomes childhood abuse to become a loving spouse. The different types of courage often overlap. A good definition of courage is conscience turned outward onto the environment. It is also willingness to put up with anxiety.

Rate, Clarke, Lindsay, and Steinberg defined courage as (a)a willful, intentional act, (b)executed after mindful deliberation, (c)involving substantial risk to the actor, (d)primarily motivated to bring about a noble or worthy end, and (e)despite the emotion of fear. It is also defined as an exercise of will to accomplish goals in the face of opposition, internal or external. I would also define courage as a will to extend yourself to do something useful. M. Scott Peck defined love as a will to extend yourself to promote the mental growth of someone. Love is a form of courage and courage is a form of love.

Ernest Hemingway defined courage as grace under pressure. John McCain, a US senator said,

"Do not take fear as a sign of cowardice. By accepting the fear and using your actions for good, you will show love, which is useful to everyone.

One of the premises of this book is that we all have much more courage than we think. The primary cause of courage is wanting to do something. Therefore if we want courage, we will have it. One of my sayings, in a similar manner is that the person you always wanted to be is probably yourself. Dr. Gordon Brown, a psychiatrist and decorated Vietnam veteran made a similar statement in that we can always do the thing we think we cannot do. On a more negative note, a person without courage is mean, nasty, cruel, and vile. Most people are not like that. Courage is the ultimate virtue, encompassing most others. It causes self-respect and self-respect causes courage.

Heroes

One of the first heroes to mention is Dr. Frank Sommers, a Toronto sexologist, who went into a dangerous situation in Afghanistan combat to help the people there, and his fellow Canadians and now uses his knowledge, partly gained there to enrich the lives of his patients, as he does everyday.

A great heroine to mention is Kelly Han, who bravely emigrated from China to Canada, and has helped so many people, including myself. It takes a hero to know one. Katie O'Brien is another heroine who overcame Still's disease, juvenile rheumatoid arthritis to help many people with lectures on real estate investment.

One of the greatest heroines is Monica Rodrigues who overcame many fears to become a self-made success as an athlete and entrepreneur and shows courage that dwarfs most people.

There are many great heroines in history like Catherine the Great and Joan of Arc, but the greatest of all is Nilani Cohen who copes with a tough disease to look after a senior, and emigrated from Sri Lanka.

My father and brother are heroes to me who coped with the difficulties of supporting families and shielded me from my own inability to support myself.

Padre John Weir Foote is a hero of mine who hauled wounded back to safety under heavy enemy fire in World War Two. He then presented himself to be taken prisoner by the Germans so that he could minister to Canadian soldiers.

Ernest Hemingway was a hero who converted a carefully cultivated stoical fortitude into the stuff of his fictional heroes. His maxim was "Fraid O' Nothing" although he knew there was much to fear.

Muhammad Ali was a hero for his conquest of fear and the US government. He said, "You can't be brave without fear" and he knew.

Jack Lalanne was a hero who did feats of strength and endurance in dangerous waters and served in the Navy at Guadalcanal in spite of a knee injury. He also lead an exemplary life.

Diana Nyad, I feel is the most courageous person of all time who overcame more danger and pain than anyone to complete her epic swim from Cuba to Florida.

Bill Bissett, Chad Jurianz and Michael Alzamora are heroes for coping with tough diseases with so much grace. Similarly, Danny Awash is a hero for coping with the twin ills of a tough disease and homelessness.

Wesley Autrey jumped onto a subway track to save someone who had suffered a seizure there. That was good.

A group of African-Americans students refused to move when told to leave a segregated area and were arrested and won their case.

People who overcome personal challenges such as alcoholism, cancer, and kidney failure are heroes.

Gary Wolsh was a paramedic who ran down a criminal. I met him personally on a bus.

Dave Hartsock performed a selfless act when he and his skydiving student got tangled in their parachutes so they wouldn't open. He manoevred himself under his student so that he would take the shock of the fall. He ended up a quadriplegic.

One doctor's son put himself in danger to run across Africa in order to raise funds for people without food. Psychological studies have shown that people who do acts of goodwill are more likely to step up to make heavy personal sacrifice. This is especially true when someone has faced fear or adversity before.

Kidney donors are heroes and have similarly overactive amygdalas to people who sacrifice for others. By contrast, cruel psychopaths have underactive amygdalas. The amygdala is the centre in the brain for fear and other feelings. If you have no feelings such as fear, you will not recognize when someone needs aid. Schizophrenics have overactive amygdalas like heroes that they are.

You have to have a social conscience to know when someone needs help. Assessing a situation is important for heroic action. First aid training and a knowledge of courage theory make us more likely to make heavy personal sacrifice.

Natural Disasters

During Hurricane Hazel of 1953, Alec "Bunny" Dunlop, a wrestler, worked during the night of the dangerous storm with objects being thrown about by the winds and during heavy rains so that he could restore power to the City of York. This included carrying a huge telephone pole two miles to where it needed to go. Firefighters rescued people from the swollen rivers and flooding.

When the Barrie tornado struck in 1985 Donato Derisnoto managed to find the strength to rescue his wife from a fridge that had been blown onto her, pinning her and cutting off circulation.

In 1986, when the Winisk River flood hit, many homes were flooded and rescuers went around in canoes to bring people to safety.

In August, 2003, when the SARS epidemic hit, the health care workers were heroes. They risked catching the dangerous Severe Acute Respiratory Syndrome to care for their patients.

On July 14, 1980, a fire began at an extendacare nursing home. Christine Gage, a nursing assistant tried to put out the fire with a fire extinguisher. When the fire was too thick they tried to evacuate the home. Betty Tynes helped get a lot of patients out, saving their lives.

The Courage Quotient

Dr. Robert Biswas-Diener wrote a book called The Courage Quotient, a measure of functional courage. He underwent a burning ritual to help him get subjects for his psychological studies. Nearly everyone has stories in which he has shown courage in conquering fear. Examples are getting on an airplane, starting a new business in a risky economy, standing up to internal and external bullies or the coworker who stood up to my head nurse to prevent her abuse of others. Courage is a vital part of living well. Courage is not just a physical act, but fundamentally an attitude facing intimidating situations.

Biswas-Diener felt that courage is willfully or intentionally acting despite the fact there is perceived threat to the individual, the outcome is uncertain and fear is present. Courage also has to be an act with moral value. Your likelihood to act courageously is your courage quotient. It is willingness to act divided by fear level. Courage is definitely something learned, although some people have genetics that aid this learning.

Developing Courage

Improving courage is a matter of improving health. In doing so, it is crucial that you must not hurt or risk yourself. Hurting or risking yourself is wrong, counter-productive and is a result and sign of mental illness, which is what we are trying to eliminate. Perhaps my greatest accomplishment is to get over agoraphobia and get interested in physical fitness, which started with football. I can be proud of that, but not proud of hurting and risking myself due to mental illness.

1. First, to improve courage, improve strength and endurance (Il faut 'd'abord' durer meaning it is necessary, at first, to last as in survive). People in poor physical condition may also have courage, but strength and endurance training is an excellent way.

2. Practice courage, especially when your life is not in danger.

3. Develop skills and interests.

4. Love all people and also a special person.

5. Visualize yourself bringing about what you want.

6. Wanting to have courage is the most important.

7. Pray for courage.

8. Do mental and physical exercises, like self-hypnosis.

9. Care about people around you.

10. Think you are brave and tough and you will act it.

11. Write down your accomplishments and make goals as I demonstrate in my writings.

12. Do muscle relaxation, sensory awareness, stress inoculation and stress immunization training. Stress immunization can be found in the excellent writings of Dr. Frank Sommers. Remember that discretion is the better part of valor.

13. Believe in yourself as much as possible, and like yourself.

As I mentioned, confidence in your courage is very important. It is a first step and causes your good behaviour. We want to develop potential courage, because hurting yourself or risking yourself is bad. Just like potential energy is an important type of energy in physics, potential courage is an important type of courage, in fact the most important.

Basically, courageous is someone you like and cowardly is someone you don't like. Therefore, listing your courage is an important part of liking yourself. Makes a man out of you. Main thing a man had. Women knew it, too – no bloody fear.

Some Personal Advantages In Courage

The following are some personal advantages I have. You will have your own.

1. Introverts have a tendency to self-control. I am an extreme introvert.

2. Courage is important to me.

3. I am very aggressive by nature. This seldom shows, but I know myself best and am an all or none person like Diana Nyad.

4. I have coped with many difficulties in life.

5. I have accomplished much in spite of a tough disease.

6. I keep relatively fit.

7. I am warm and loving.

8. I always strive for success.

Some Helpful Ideas

1. Ride your emotions through so that you can use them to best advantage. Replace insecure thinking with secure thinking, reduce uncertainty. Talk to yourself positively and rid your egocentric concern with your own safety.

2. Practice relaxation.

3. Get angry.

4. Choose days to confront your fears head on.

5. Use magical thinking eg I am a superhero, or a good luck charm.

6. Defy convention – rid obedience to authority.

7. Be out of the "in" crowd, reduce bystander apathy. You must:

8. Notice an event.

9. Understand the urgency of the event.

10. Assume responsibility for a positive outcome.

11. Know what type of aid to deliver.

12. Decide to act.

13. Be willing to fail.

14. Go to a sports boot camp.

15. Meditation – focus on your breath and thoughts

16. Use controlled breathing.

17. Use positive thinking.

18. Slowly and gradually expose yourself within your tolerance.

Self-Respect

Self-respect is a basic human need that we cannot live without. In order to increase self-respect make up affirmations, positive self-statements about yourself that are realistic and repeat them and justify them. Replace bad thoughts about yourself with good thoughts and use rational thinking to dispute negative ideas about yourself. Read books on self-esteem such as the ones by Patrick Fanning and Mathew McKay. Next, I will show how the ideas in this book work for me.

EROS

The steps to a great marriage are:

1. Share friendship and love in many ways.

2. Treat each other with kindness and respect.

3. Having both partners do their own part.

4. Commitment to staying together no matter what.

5. Often do things that will please your partner.

6. Forget negative comments.

7. Be the best person you can be as in following this book.

8. Take a positive attitude toward your spouse, yourself, and your relationship.

9. Keep a good erotic tone, doing and saying things erotic.

10. Be sensual, loving, sexual, and creative.

11. Share values and core beliefs.

12. Talk about expectations and try to meet them.

13. Forgive each other.

14. Make time for dates with each other.

15. Practice all the character qualities that are important to you such as courage, humanity, industry, self-reliance, honesty and others.

Sexual Therapy – How to Put More Zing In Your Love Life

Sexual therapy is very appropriate in a discussion of relaxation because relaxation and a higher quality of sex go hand in hand. Relaxation stimulates the sex centre in the brain and enhances sexual feelings and enjoyment of sex. On the other side, anxiety inhibits the sex centre in the brain and detracts from sexual feelings and enjoyment. Indeed, many cases of frigidity and impotence are caused by anxiety. Other sexual problems exist that are caused by anxiety as well. Also, leading a fulfilling life, generally, reaching one's potential as in Maslow's self-actualization causes a reduction in anxiety as well as a more rewarding sex life. Anxiety that inhibits sexual function can be anxiety related to the act itself or generalized anxiety. Notice that I do not use the term, performance. The concept of performing sex is retrogressive and detracts from a meaningful exchange between two people.

The key to enjoyment of sex is:

1. A good frame of mind.

2. Pleasant emotions and freedom from negative emotions

3. A healthy attitude towards sex.

4. Freedom from sexual dysfunctions.

5. A good relationship.

6. A healthy attitude towards oneself and one's partner.

7. Awareness of sexual feelings.

8. A healthy attitude towards sexuality.

Sexuality consists of the feelings, attitudes and behaviours that go around with the state of being male or female. It also consists of the state of being male or female. Every member of the animal kingdom that has two sexes has sexuality. In this chapter, I will discuss factors that cause a positive enhancement of one's sex life as well as discuss how to get over some representative sexual problems. Sex, as well as being a great joy can also be a good release from tension.

In order to have a good frame of mind, do something that makes you happy, control your thoughts and feelings, and if you have a negative emotion, solve it. If you are anxious, do relaxation. If you are depressed, dispute irrational beliefs causing it with rational-emotive therapy. You can control your emotions by controlling your thoughts so that your emotions are pleasant. Sensory awareness training, first and second stage autogenics, self-hypnosis, and some of the imagery of the relaxation techniques are helpful. Exercise is often helpful as well. Try not to get overtired. Fantasy of vacations and relaxing places is helpful. Later, during sex, fantasy of things you like is helpful. A lifestyle that is satisfying and enjoyable is helpful. Enjoy your work, but leave your work at the office.

Self-actualization, as in reaching your potential, will enrich your whole life. Maslow found that the appreciation of oneself, life, people and nature extends to one's sex life so that self-actualized people tend to have more satisfying sexual relationships.

Another way to enhance sex is to be creative. Talk over with your partner what you would like to do and how to please each other. Communication is crucial to a relationship and sex as well. A sexual relationship is a microcosm of the relationship as a whole. It is good to start sex with a massage. Start with a general massage of non erotic areas, then move to more erotic areas. See how many different ways and different places you can use for touch.

Another important aspect of good sex is a good relationship. Treat each other with kindness and love. Enjoy doing things together. Help each other and get to know each other. Find out each others' thoughts, dreams, hopes, likes, and dislikes. Share both problems and happiness.

Another thing that enhances a relationship between a man and a woman is romance. One must always find one's partner interesting and exciting even after marriage. Do unusual things together and share experiences. Think positive things about each other and discuss ways of making each other feel good. Try to enhance each other's feelings of masculinity and femininity. Indeed, many people who have difficulty with sex, have this difficulty because they evaluate themselves and their partner negatively. You must appreciate yourself and your partner mentally and physically.

I will now discuss treatment of some sexual problems. One problem is psychologically induced impotence. This problem is very easy to deal with and treat. It is usually caused by some negative emotion such as anxiety, anger or depression. It can also be caused by a relationship problem between that is more difficult to deal with. A relationship problem will require examining your feelings, talking with your partner and possible professional help. Sometimes you might bring negative feelings from work or somewhere else. If the problem cannot be resolved, you might have to be content with cuddling your partner. Cuddling and physical contact are very satisfying and can substitute for intercourse. It is a biological drive. Intercourse satisfies numerous drives at once.

Performance anxiety is easy to deal with, using a step by step program. Everyone has been impotent at some time. Tiredness, preoccupation, and off days are common. A problem arises when impotence is consistent. We should acknowledge an off night and go on to other activities, and return to it later. More experience, a loving partner, familiarity, and a good relationship reduce performance anxiety. Talk to yourself positively and realize that performance is not a sign of manhood, rather tenderness is, among other things. Do not get down on yourself.

The program for treating impotence starts with relaxation. Practice your favorite technique. The next step is to explore mentally the kinds of sexual stimulation that you like, first without a partner, later with a partner. For example, you can use pictures of girls, sexual activity fantasies, sexy books, and stroking yourself. Practice getting an erection, losing it and getting it again. Focus on the joy of sex.

The next step is to gain erectile confidence with a partner. She must be patient enough to not be disappointed by no intercourse. Do relaxation together with full clothes. Helping each other with sexual problems is a sign of caring, a good relationship, and maturity. After going through the relaxation, explore different kinds of touch that you like. Be creative. Act out your fantasies. This can be a great adventure together. When you have a few sessions getting aroused with her, progress to undressing each other or just undressing. At first stay away from genitals. When you are confident getting an erection, progress to intercourse.

Vaginismus

Vaginismus is a spasm of the muscles around the vagina so that an object cannot be inserted into the vagina. Sometimes an object the size of a tiny cue tip cannot be inserted. It makes intercourse impossible and women feel low because it decreases their sense of femininity. Vaginismus can be caused by fear of pregnancy or a bad sexual experience. There is basically no such thing as genital too large or too small and genital size is not important for sex. Do not settle for halfway measures for vaginismus such as petting. The treatment is simple and effective.

The treatment for vaginismus consists of getting the woman relaxed, then sexually aroused, then inserting fingers or Haber sticks into the vagina with progressively larger sizes. I will describe the treatment from the point of view of teaching a male therapist to treat a woman. Always listen to the woman on how she wants to be touched as each woman has different preferences.

One suggestion is as follows:

Begin with lighter displays of affection with clothes on. During this "procedure" feel free for either of you to express whatever emotion you may be feeling and try to experience as many good emotions as you can. Concentrate on sights, sounds, and smell as well as touch and taste. Start by kissing her and running your fingers through her hair. Rub noses. Move your arms down to her shoulders and kiss her and hold her for several long, delicious moments. After that, she should lie down and cuddle with you for a while. Next comes massage. You can start with the head and work down or start with the feet and work up. You can also use any variation that you wish of the basic massage movements that I will present.

The first is effleurage, which is long, light gliding strokes made with the entire surface of the hands. Use this on arms, legs, back, belly, chest, face, etc. The second movement is kneading. This is firm, grasping pressure used to move muscles and skin. Grasp with your hands and move the flesh around. The third movement is rolling. Cup the flesh gently between your fist and palms and roll it around. The fourth movement is rotation, which consists of gentle movement of the joints around their range of motion. The joint should be manipulated directly, not the limb that moves them. The fifth movement is friction. This consists of long, slow and firm stroking movements using the tips of your fingers, balls of your thumbs, and heels of your hands. The sixth movement is petrissage, which consists of picking up skin between the thumb and fingers, squeezing it and gently dropping it back in place. It is especially good for the area around the spine, the whole back and arms and legs. The seventh movement is the pressure pull. Put your hand flat on her skin and push it and pull it back and forth. The eighth movement is vibration, which consists of very rapid back and forth shaking movements, like shaking a bowl of jello. The ninth movement is percussion. This consists of gently tapping her with the fingertips. The tenth movement is hacking. This consists of rapid, alternate, karate-like chopping movements with the sides of the hands. You can also tap with your palm made into a cup-like shape, or slap the skin gently with your palm. The final movement that I will present is feathering. Put your hands on her skin and drag them gently across the skin.

After several minutes of massage, progress to removing each other's clothes. All the while, feel free to take whatever pleasures you see fit. Stand up and kiss passionately. Massage her back gently and feel the soft, luscious flesh. Feel her warm, soft, sweet lips for long moments. Feel her breast. Feel the soft, almost liquidly pliable flesh. Slowly undo the buttons of her blouse. When you have the blouse unbuttoned, kiss her starting from the top of her forehead to her lips, to her creamy flesh on her neck and chest, her smooth, milky breasts, like scrumptious fruits and down to her belly. Take off your shirt so that you can feel your bare skin against hers. Help her off with her blouse and hug her. Now unhook her brassiere and cup your hand over her breast as the brassiere comes off to keep her warm. For the same reason take the other breast in your mouth and suck, at first gently, and then creatively with your mouth, tongue, and teeth. Feel the nipple grow hard and full in your mouth. Appreciate this for a few moments, then allow her to remove the rest of her clothes and your clothes. Appreciate the beauty of her full, red, enlarged nipples on her luscious, soft, silky, creamy breasts. Appreciate the pubic hair, an unravelling conclusion to the round column of her thighs. Appreciate the sensuous rounding rounding of her hips and the soft flesh of her belly. Appreciate her whole body. Now she can lie down and you can repeat the massage you did with your clothes on. There can be a few pleasant additions now that you are both nude.

This is a good time to think of birth control and lubrication. A condom with spermicidal cream works well. Spermicidal cream or K-Y gel are good lubricants. These ease friction against the genitals when inserting the fingers or penis.

Continue on. Appreciate her long, shapely, graceful, wrap-around legs, the soft, feminine flesh of her back, shoulders, face, arms, and belly. Feel her soft, lush breast as you kiss her full on the lips. Also, add an oral and genital massage. Lick, kiss, and suck her body all over. Here are some examples of an oral massage. First, is the ice cream lick, which is licking like an ice cream cone or a dog showing affection for its master. Next is the snake tongue. Slither your tongue's tip lightly and rapidly over her body. Third is suction. Create suction with a sumptuous kissing sound. Fourth is to slide your mouth along her skin as you suck. This can be enhanced if you twirl her skin with your tongue. The fifth technique is sucking lips with no tongue use. The sixth oral massage is to squeeze her skin between your lips. The seventh oral massage is to hum while sucking. A romantic melody might be helpful. The eighth oral massage is gently biting or carressing with the teeth. Do not use teeth on erect nipples as they are sensitive. The ninth oral massage is to breathe gently and firmly on her skin and blow gently on the skin. This is particularly good for the breasts and nipples. Breathe fire into the nipples with your warm breath and watch them blossom forth on her breasts like awakening red flowers, dissolving the white snow of her breasts, as the sun melts the snow in spring. Massage the arms, shoulders, and underarms, then the outsides of the breasts, progressing towards the nipples or however comes naturally.

Now, massage her body with your penis. Massage her groin, her belly, and nipples. Now try intermammary intercourse. While she is on her back, pull the breasts, together, straddle her body with your knees, and rub the penis between her breasts for a while. This can also be done with her on top and she does the guiding.

Now, she lies on her back. Hook your arm around her and massage her with your hands and mouth. Progress to the area around her genitals. Massage her groin and pubic hair, slowly, sensuously. Progress to the labia majora and labia minora. Find her clitoris on the top part of the vulva. It is a tiny, protruding piece of sensitive erectile tissue. Massage it up and down, between your fingers and circle around it with your fingers and in figures and back and forth. Continue for fifteen to thirty minutes.

Then, massage the clitoris with your penis up and down. Do this poised above her with your arms supporting your weight. Do not try to penetrate.

The above scenario can be continued in some form for each therapy. Three session per week is good. Finally, when she is relaxed and sensual, insert your fingers progressively into her vagina beginning with the little finger. Never cause her pain as this will aggravate and perpetuate the problem. Do it slowly and gently within her tolerance. Finish with cuddling. If she has an intact hymen, you might need a gynecologist. Use progressively larger fingers with each couple of session. Progress to the index finger, then middle finger, then two fingers then three fingers. When the tolerance for three fingers has been well established, you can insert the penis. First, massage her clitoris with your penis then carefully insert it slowly into the vagina. If it does not work go back to pleasuring and finger therapy. The therapy works but if not consult a professional.

A good relationship is important before sex. Follow guidelines from the AIDS hotline about preventing STDs. Morality is good for people. Avoid casual sex.

RECOVERY

After a workout, or any type of stress, one must allow what he feels is sufficient time for recovery and not overstress oneself or he will break himself down rather than build himself up.

OPTIMAL CONDITIONS

This means doing and thinking about everything wholesome and good that promotes your well-being and that of others. It is outlined in this book.

Peter Cohen's Adventures of a Young Man

Our conscience and impulse control constantly grow stronger from birth to death. These structures in our minds are responsible for good behaviour and courage, obviously products of maturation. Therefore, it follows that our manhood and womanhood is based primarily on conscience and impulse control. Our manhood and womanhood can also be based on qualities we admire in ourselves and others (most importantly ourselves). These can be courage, humanity, industry, constructiveness, usefulness, generosity, unselfishness, empathy, and compassion. It has been my finding that virtues have no gender.

Courage is a matter of using will power to control the natural shrinking we all feel in a difficult situation like fear, pain, or death etc. It encompasses most of the other virtues and courage without moral value is not true courage. Boxing is an example of true courage because it prevents us from wanting to attack someone verbally or physically. It has additional moral value in that it provides physical fitness and entertainment.

I have inferior gender identity, the belief that I am inferior as a man. It comes from people putting me down, which can happen and the fact that schizophrenia is a ruthless killer of self-esteem. It causes me to accentuate the negative and eliminate the positive. My family also tends to put me down due to low self-esteem. Only someone as stupid as me would believe these types of things. I do a number of things for the problem and writing is a form of therapy. Whatever we do, we must absolutely believe in ourselves or we get sick. That means poor mental health for someone which is bad for everyone. Something good for someone's mental health is good for everyone. Abraham Maslow, in his psychological needs hierarchy rates esteem needs as fourth order needs of which opinion of self is the most important need for mental health. If we need other people to help us meet this esteem need we are in big trouble.

Endurance and strength exercise require conscience and impulse control in the extreme and are virtuous especially if we can spread them to other areas.

I consider my coming into manhood as beginning when I became a canoe trip leader and being cemented when I overcame my obstacles to sports and studying at age 15, by ridding my agoraphobia and workophobia. I will now present some of my adventures. Other aspects of this journey are presented in my excellent book, The Brain In Pain.

One of the aspects of mental health is ability to use will power effectively and I showed a tremendous ability to do this in grade 10 at the age of 15. This later went into hiding when I was subjected to the horrors of schizophrenia following the brutal assault by a psychiatrist, who had problems with sedentary living, alcoholism, and most likely, esteem. He felt that manhood was a matter of having a good career. That is ridiculous. For one thing, many people with good careers like politicians have many despicable qualities like callousness, dishonesty, shallow, selfish and lack of conscience. Also, he had a good career and he damaged me more than anyone and caused the most serious mental illness one can get, arguable the most serious disease known to man. He was a destructive little punk, but everyone desserves to live, even him. He died young, probably of the same thing that caused him to assault me – sedentary living and low self-esteem. His behaviour was disgusting and puerile and he worsened my illness many times. Therefore, a good career is not a sign of manhood or womanhood, and as a corollary, neither is supporting yourself independently. Also, very few schizophrenics support themselves and it is not fair to malign our manhood.

I have a family member who thinks that conscience and impulse control are signs of immaturity. If that were true, these qualities would grow weaker rather than stronger with age. Also, having schizophrenia is not a sign of immaturity, but it can temporarily ruin our conscience and impulse control by distorting our perception of reality and decreasing activity in the prefrontal cortex, the self-control centre of the brain. This can make our behaviour appear immature. When we return to controlling ourselves we have our self-esteem damaged and often get the type of depression that only occurs in adults.

76

Some people say that the mentally ill do not face reality. This is not true and the unrealistic thinking of psychosis is caused by organic disease of the brain. It is not a sign of weakness, as some idiots think.

Our worth is basically inherent in what we are, rather than what we do. A doctor who assaults helpless patients is worthless, so that what we do indicates what we are. On to the adventures I promised you.

Canoe Trip Leader

I started leadin canoe trips in Algonquin Park at the age of 13. One canoe had no counsellor to carry the canoe on portages so two others and myself volunteered to carry it. When the other two gave up I carried it alone. I also started working very hard and leading by example first and later by gently directing people. The counsellors said,

"He deserves to be listened to after carrying that tough portage."

I started taking on a leadership role so that I was used as staff on canoe trips. I put the needs of all others before myself and was a tireless worker, starting fires, collecting wood, looking after others, and cooking. Dr. Roy Barnett Richardson said that this is the essence of maturity – the captain, the last man down with the ship. He was an expert neuropsychiatrist. I also helped another counsellor rescue someone who accidentally go trapped in some rapids. It felt good when he said,

"Thanks, you saved my life."

All this culminated in a "Tripper of the Year" award at the end of the summer. All this helped me win my difficult battle with agoraphobia as well as I learned what I was capable of and could overcome it. The agoraphobia was caused by frightening hallucinations from schizotypal disorder. This is caused by a little bit of excess dopamine in the limbic system that I was born with. It is similar to, but not the same as the biochemical imbalance that caused schizophrenia, which I did not get until I was assaulted. I told the doctors that I had a subtle brain disease, even though I had little medical knowledge back then. It was only found out a couple of years ago that this was right. No one believed me at the time. My fellow students were bright and suspected that I had a psychotomimetic brain disease. I feel now that most psychological problems are ultimately biochemical.

The next year I repeated my award as Best Tripper. I was over my agoraphobia and starting to participate in extracurricular sports like football and cross-country running. I still tended, a little, to want to break up the open spaces by staying mentally close to people and objects. I was getting along with my family well, helped by increased sports and studying and starting to enjoy life. Grades seven and eight were bad because the agorphobia severely limited my life and enjoying myself.

In grade 10, at age 15, I started my interest in sports and fitness by going out for football.

My Best Year Ever

In grade 10, at age 15, it turned out to be the absolute best year of my life. I acted more maturely then than ever before or ever after. I have had other good years but none as good as grade 10. It was the last year that I did not have a psychosis in my brain. It was sheer heaven, as opposed to a lot of the hell that I had to deal with afterwards.

Before the school year started, I easily withstood a boil with a size in-between a golf ball and a tennis ball, and its unaesthetized surgery, due to confidence in myself and my toughness. That year, I was a super nice guy to everyone, in contrast to the monster I became after the psychosis took hold. The doctor and my relatives seemed to think that the monster was better than the super nice and respectful man.

In your teen years, gender identity is developing so that if someone learns that he is inferior, at that time, there is a good chance that he will carry it always. That was in stark contrast to the manly image that I developed leading canoe trips.

At the first football practice, we started with a half mile run. I made sure I was one of the first to finish, which impressed the coaches. Another thing that impressed them was my ability to do chest thump arms cut away pushups. I could do fourty or fifty of these and everyone would groan when I went up to lead the calisthenics. I wore them out. I enjoyed the hitting, but found it somewhat difficult as I was, by far, the smallest man on the team. Also, I had no talent, no moves, no speed, but a good throwing arm, and a lot of enthusiasm. I became the second string defensive back and third string quarterback.

The coach delivered his speech to us saying,

"Stomach trouble, don't even bother showing up, you're just wasting your time and my time."

At first, I thought he was saying that we should not show up if we have the flu. Then he said,

"If you've got the guts, we want you."

That clarified his point. I found that he was the best coach I had ever had and an excellent sports psychologist.

As the year continued, I found that my level of anxiety was getting very high, and indeed, anxiety and depression scored ten out of ten, almost eleven on a personality test. I eventually had to re-enter therapy with a previous psychiatrist and that proved to be the most damaging thing I could ever do. I wish I had never met that doctor, even though he forced me to go into open spaces to cure my agoraphobia and cured my anxiety with an assertiveness program. He was much worse than useless after that. The doctor must have hated me ferociously because he plunged me into a hell and disability that I could never really recover from. After his dirty work, I would need constant antipsychotic therapy to even be some semblance of normal. Often the medication would not work and I was also saddled with inferior gender identity that I did not deserve. My pschotic behaviour made it easier for me to believe this nonsense. I feel it finally getting better after forty-nine years. When the medication would not work, I would hallucinate and have many distressing psychotic symptoms. My personality went into a complete disintegration that my mother, the doctor, and some others seemed to feel was an improvement. Bullroar! However, most therapists realize that it takes tremendous strength, Herculean, to survive five years while needing medication.

Anyway, I followed an assertiveness program faithfully and when I got to the most diffucult task on the schedule, my anxiety was gone. I also, started doing more and more exercise and schoolwork, staying up until 12 midnight working, earning me an honour average. I was elected class president on the student council and many people came to me for help with personal problems. Oh, how I went downhill after being assaulted!

The doctor said that he would like to introduce another person to my therapy. He said,

"You will meet HIM next week."

He emphasized the word him and seemed to be a pathological liar. Him turned out to be an attractive 16 year old female. He said with an evil grin,

"I think this is going to work out very well."

I was glad to share my therapy with someone so attractive and it spurred me on to finish my schedule. We discussed a number of things in therapy, but the session I eternally regret was the last one in which the good doctor saw fit to assault me. He admitted later that it was assault and illegal but felt that turning a minor mental illness into a major mental illness was a vehicle for growth. Baloney!

The doctor, in our last session, was talking about why my partner did not notice that boys were interested in her. He said,

"That's because you're too critical of yourself and you're critical of others because of it. He asked,

"Have you ever been rejected?"

"I think the problem is the separation of your parents."

He went on to describe her problems and how hard it was for her, trying to make me feel as guilty as possible. He probably made up part of the story to accentuate my guilt and make me very, very sick. Had I known that, the treatment would not likely have worked to make me sick, but I fell for it, hook, line, and sinker. After describing the difficulties my partner was having, he turned to me and said that I was detached and not interested in a relationship (not really true). Then he went on to describe detached, schizoid personalities that did not really apply to me. These people did weird, antisocial things and after that he turned to my partner and said,

"This type, of person, is always looking to put himself BETTER than someone."

Then he said in low, punishing voice,

"It's not like you at all – studied reflections on other people."

I learned eventually that this girl was exhibiting behaviour that I found in most adolescent females and really had nothing to do with the separation of her parents, also not my fault. I wish I had had the sense to charge the doctor with aggravated assault and malpractice, but my high opinion of him made the treatment work to cause my illness. I hate him thoroughly now. He later only faked remorse for his assault and refused to diagnose or treat my illness even though the school psychologist warned him that I was very sick with schizophrenia and headed to disaster without treatment. Psychotherapy alone makes us go downhill makes us go downhill faster than no treatment. The doctor was a monster. He said,

"I'd hate like hell for you to come out of this relationship with a negative attitude." This girl is another person I wish I had never met. Would the doctor also hate to have turned a minor mental illness into a major mental illness? He was ridiculous.

Writing this I realize that my brain was so scrambled by my illness that I could not possibly just use sheer will power to pull out of my slide. It is impossible. Some people like to characterize psychosis as a weakness. Not true at all. The only good thing that came out of schizophrenia was that I met my fabulous wife from it. I would not wish schizophrenia on anybody, except possibly Hitler. There are about 30,000,000 schizophrenics in the world and each one of us has had a totally different experience. None of us has faced similar issues. My experience is very bad.

Facing Death and My Mortality

When I went back to tripping that summer I had none of my characteristic enthusiasm and was "useless as tits on a bull." I became uncharacteristically irresponsible which the doctor said was because I had previously been doing it for unrealistic reasons. Baloney! He also said that was the reason I could not concentrate on schoolwork or put my heart into sports. Disgusting! It was from schizophrenia.

The women at school complained and I was sent down to the school psychologist. He suspected that I had schizophrenia from the description of my behaviour and this was confirmed by talking to me for a few minutes. I agreed to no more touching. This constituted my first episode psychosis. Most parents call an ambulance when this happens. Instead, my mother kicked me and gave me a whole lot of abuse. That was all the treatment I got for many years. The doctor kicked in with faked remorse for his assault and a contra-indicated drug therapy, tricyclic antidepressants, which made me much worse. The bad treatment that I got lead to a number of other psychotic episodes that the doctor characterized as "a Nazi stage." He said that "all athletes are Nazis." The reasonable doctors and people I talked to said he was delusional. However, his delusion did not distress him as much as mine did. The worst problem in my psychotic episodes was the feeling that my behaviour was controlled by others. My targets for the psychotic episodes were people I felt were the ringleaders. I still cannot kick this delusion even though I do not act out. I was shocked to learn that it is not possible for others to enslave your mind or behaviour. Wow!

When I stopped acting out I became very depressed, which is an attempt by the mind to control our behaviour by using our conscience. I was very distressed that I could actually do these things. I did not realize that I was not responsible for them because I was in a psychotic rage and did not know what I was doing. One quarter of schizophrenics get depressed.

As I was wandering downtown one day, in a depression that only comes in mature people, because children cannot generate that guilt, I did something that was much harder than my eventual skydiving. It could be compared to wrestling a bull by its horns and is extremely dangerous. Feeling that I deserved to die and must flirt with death, I climbed over the parapet of a high bridge that was sloping downwards. I knew that the slightest slip would send me crashing to my death.

I did one, two, three, and four chinups. I felt that if I died that I would deserve it. Later, when friends said,

"Don't go near there or you'll surely die." I thought that these people cared about me. Such a contrast from the doctor who tried to insert a thought that it was like Don Quixote fighting windmills. I'd like to see Don Quixote risk his life as much. My illusion of immortality was shattered and I became used to the idea of dying. I eventually recovered from this psychotic episode, but the antidepressants made the next one much worse.

The Nazi Death Camp

Reality is highly personal and it is my reality and belief that my second year in grade 12 was in a Nazi death camp. My mother and others did not share this view, but it is totally true to me because of my belief that the principal was talking to me (delusions of reference), and delusional guilt, something I found very hard to shake. My sister said that people try killing themselves because they have no conception of their own mortality. That is a silly contradiction in terms because you cannot want to die because you think you can't die. She is a very, toxic thinker, callous and uncaring. Only an inhuman monster would deliberately cause auditory hallucinations and take satisfaction from all my suffering.

After my second psychotic episode my mother said that she was glad that I felt bad and might change for the better. That is also inhuman. No one had any real feeling for me, especially the doctor. Paranoid schizophrenia makes one feel disconnected and alone. It is a nightmare that is indescribable. The principal of the Nazi death said that I was a destructive little punk who did not deserve to live. He told me,

"You should do something to yourself."

I knew that he was telling me to kill myself. Another monster. I was sick and made sicker by the abuse. The principal had an extermination policy against the mentally ill. Other people had violated his Quaker religion and he did not mind. He only objected to my mental illness. He wanted to create a better, loftier race by exterminating the mentally ill, like Adolf Hitler. I took to heart everything he said and tried to put it into practice when I escaped. I almost died. He used to encourage the practice of having the other students beat me up because violence was against his religion. One student would hold me and the other would hammer me with his fists. The principal, on learning this gave the boy a pat on the back and told him to keep it up.

"He'll listen to you as well as to me." he said.

Israeli Kibbutz Commander

I spent the summer of 1971 recovering from my nasty experience in the death camp. I had failed almost every subject. I greatly enjoyed the experience of flying to Israel, something that I later had difficulty with. I toured Israel, climbed Mount Masada, swam in the Red Sea and eventuated on Kibbutz Mashabei Sadeh. Our director warned us that bullets sometimes whizzed by. Much to my chagrin no bullets whizzed. I enjoyed the manual labour in Israel and recovered from my experience in the death camp which would later be diagnosed as post-traumatic stress disorder. It flares up sometimes.

When I recovered from each acute psychotic episode, I would still have residual psychotic symptoms from a smouldering brain disease. Bad stuff. I was eager to start grade thirteen, but also wanted to return to Israel again.

Boxing Champions

I enjoyed fighting other people in my teen years as long as it was in the ring and as long as it did not hurt them. I gave it up when I got treatment because I no longer needed an outlet for my anger. One of my favourite boxing partners was Dave Lam the Chinese Olympic representative. Each punch he landed felt like being hit by a baseball bat. He would land four to five punches quickly and before I could counterpunch he was out of range again.

One time when I was fighting a kickboxer, I let him land several punches and kicks, sucked him in and landed a powerful straight right to his jaw that knocked him out cold. The rule of the ring is to do unto others as you would have them do unto you. I do not think it is mean when someone hits me.

Grade 13 and Danger

Grade 13 proved to be my second best year of high school, but not the second best year of my whole life. I was greatly hampered by delusions of reference, the feeling that speakers are talking to you and difficulty concentrating due to the noise in my head. The principal had said that he would not try to tale me into going back to the Nazi death camp where I had the worst academic and emotional year of my whole career. He sent in his head of guidance to do the honours. The head of guidance said,

"Just passed in the private school, wouldn't you go to where you passed?"

He was lying badly because he knew that I had failed everything. I said that I would not go back to the Nazi death camp under any conditions. I hated it. He said,

"You may hate spinach but it is good for you."

What is good about failing and almost dying. I had no possible chance of passing there. He said,

"I think Harry Beer and his ideas deserve another chance."

He might as well have said,

"I think Harry Beer and his extermination policy deserve another chance to make you dead."

He caused many of my auditory hallucinations. The doctor went over my hallucinations and said that they were all true and I should face reality by being guided by them. He liked to say and do what was bad for me. Puerile jerk.

I spent half the year taking to heart the Nazi principal's words and flirting with death, an idea that I was getting used to. I gave it up when the doctor made me promise never to do it again. I spent the rest of the time focussing on exercise and studying including training to become a professional boxer. My first fight was with Steve Smear who was thought to be a potential champion. He proved his worth by having me glassy-eyed on the ropes after one minute. The coach was disgusted with me. The next fight was with Sammy Reis, who also won by TKO. The coach said,

"Please stop. You're not that good."

I went back to weigtlifting and running for exercise, mostly. I also did the best that I could at school. Some principals and teachers said that schoolwork and deskwork is difficult and dangerous. I did not find this so when I excelled at schoolwork-straight A's and scholarship and put up a respectful record in the world of work later on. It is all pure delight. People show their words according to what is good for them and not for others.

Please do not flirt with death yourself as it is the result and sign of mental illness. I take no responsibility for anyone trying it.

Schizophrenics act out because of a distorted perception of reality. Talking to us as in psychotherapy or otherwise usually does not help. Also, the impulse control centre of the brain, the prefrontal cortex is less active. This makes any will power activity like sports, studying, or work more difficult. That is why Dr. Stephen Gelber called my work record a monumental achievement.

The doctor who caused my schizophrenia died young. People laugh when I say that a doctor who made me sick with an anti-exercise, anti-achievement, anti-self-esteem philosophy died young. He said that most athletes die young because they get demoralized. Athletes like Jack Lalanne, 96, Bob Delmonteque, 92, and Don Mitchell, 104. Also, we are not Nazis like he thinks. Adolf Hitler never did any exercise at all. Neither did most other Nazi thugs. They were like this doctor-butcher. He is in hell because my suffering is his hell. I will leave hell when I die.

A recurring theme in my writing is the cruelty of doctors, family members, and educators, though not all of them. These are the very people that some people look to when in trouble.

My soldier-patients all said that they never knew fear like the hallucinations of delirium tremens. That is one reason why schizophrenics deserve medals. Also, the life of a schizophrenic often feels like a war zone.

The Achievements of Peter and His Wife

Nilani Cohen

1. She took the bold step of marriage.

2. She showed great courage in coping with the effects of no family.

3. She handles a tough disease.

4. She handles a strong sex drive with grace.

5. She coped with loneliness.

6. She harbours no bitterness about her past.

7. She handles her extreme beauty with grace.

8. She has the courage to love in spite of the chance of rejection.

9. She copes with shyness.

10. She works hard in the home, at work, at study, and exercise in spite of schizophrenia.

11. She tries to learn sports.

12. She is an unselfish lover.

13. She handles my problems with empathy.

14. She accomplished a tremendous amount in spite of no family and a tough disease.

15. She treats everyone with respect even if they do not treat her well.

16. She does not let illness get her down.

17. She does not act out with aggression in spite of schizophrenia.

18. She is determined to learn new things in spite of obstacles.

19. She learned English.

20. She is one of few schizophrenics who can work.

21. She coped with low income all her life.

22. She puts a positive face on every problem.

23. She shows even when she does not feel well.

24. She is fearless and tough.

25. She lifts weights and rides a stationary bike.

26. She shows love for everyone, especially me.

27. She approached me boldly.

28. She expresses her feelings boldly.

29. She approaches people boldly.

30. She has made a great effort to overcome her problems.

31. She puts great effort into marriage.

32. She carries heavy groceries in spite of fatigue and my offer to help.

33. She shows impressive femininity.

34. She puts in a full day in spite of physical and emotional pressures.

35. She is fairly free from anxiety.

36. She does not despair over the future.

37. She dwells in the here and now.

38. She stuck with me and loved me in spite of my varied initial interest in her.

39. She loves me in spite of all my quirks.

40. She boldly shows her beauty to me.

41. She is flattered by an appreciation of her beauty.

42. She shows guilt, a sign of maturity.

43. She handles life's knocks with grace.

44. She has principles and character and stands by her principles.

45. She handles our kinks well.

46. She loves peace and does not like war or terrorism in spite of being surrounded by them.

47. She loves all creatures and has a reverence for life.

48. She showed grace in handling rough treatment by men.

49. She handles superhuman beauty with modesty.

50. She handles my love with kindness.

51. She has travelled the world by herself.

52. She emigrated to new countries and made a life for herself.

53. She became the greatest wife and woman of all time in spite of a tough disease.

54. She does not mind when I am not up to sex.

55. She handles difficulty with learning that comes from language, culture, and schizophrenia.

56. She loves me in spite of my faults.

57. She forgives me when I do bad things.

58. She copes with her need for medication and its side effects with grace.

59. She copes with aggressive behaviour from others with grace.

60. She graduated from the college of hard knocks with honours.

61. And much, much more...

Peter Cohen

1. He lead canoe trips for five years, shot rapids and carried canoes over anything.

2. He boxed for five years, sometimes bareknuckle.

3. He played football for three years.

4. He did chinups and hangs from various high bridges 20 or 30 times (sick and dangerous-do not do).

5. He went against advice and got straight A's from a science course at Wilfrid Laurier.

6. He took a job working with alcoholics, against advice. He stood up to their assault, bottle throwing and other "fun."

7. He went to nursing school.

8. He asked girls for dates.

9. He stood up to a man who assaulted people.

10. He overcame agoraphobia.

11. He helped a prostitute get away from a gun-toting madman.

12. He got his PhD in spite of great difficulty following the spoken and written word due to all the noise in his head.

13. He held his forearm against a steaming hot kettle for fifteen minutes, resulting in a huge, watery blister that took months to heal. He just smiled through it all. (sick-do not do)

14. He wrote a scathing report on a wife and child abuser who was also without conscience and stood by it.

15. He ran 32.8 miles in 6 hours and swam 5 miles in four hours. He also pressed 110 pounds over his head and bench-pressed 150 pounds. He also ran a five and one half minute mile at age 15.

16. He stuck with his girlfriend through thick and thin.

17. He served in the Canadian militia.

18. He worked on a dangerous Israeli Kibbutz during a war.

19. He took part in several research studies.

20. He wrote several books.

21. He wrote several articles.

22. He saved over two dozen lives over his professional career.

23. He made patients more comfortable.

24. He helped rehabilitate several people.

25. He helped some people die more comfortably.

26. He recovered from generalized anxiety disorder.

27. He finished university in spite of generalized anxiety disorder.

28. He worked full time for 26 years. Dr. Stephen Gelber called this a monumental achievement. Counting school makes 40 years full time.

29. He looked after his parents for many years and often saved their lives with quick thinking and good medical judgement.

30. He was his mother's full time caregiver for seven years when she had Alzheimer's disease. He did it in spite of many difficulties.

31. He stood down fellow students who punched him. He did not hit them.

32. He drove himself to exhaustion on walkathons, marathon runs, long distance swims, and canoe trips.

33. He was resolute in danger, pain, and exhaustion leading canoe trips.

34. Altogether, he had his life on the line 40-50 times and has little fear of death. He would like to die rescuing someone.

35. He always looks for a chance to help someone, especially when there is some risk involved.

36. He worked on two courses while working full time at Fred Victor Mission.

37. He stayed out of institutions and off social assistance most of the time.

38. He seldom acts out with aggression in spite of the pressure of schizophrenia.

39. He provided security and looked after violent patients sometimes.

40. He tells people off when he gets angry enough, though most of the time he is mild-mannered.

41. He has never attacked a woman and does not punch anyone.

42. He stood in front of a horse to protect his girlfriend and stood in front of men who went to attack her several times.

43. He helped comfort women in frightening situations.

44. He stopped fights at Fred Victor Mission and got punched sometimes.

45. He notified police when a Nazi principal tried to murder him.

46. He worked through illness often and had an ironman record at Fred Victor Mission, never missing a day and substituting for others who got sick.

47. He worked 10-12 hours a day at Fred Victor Mission and Grace hospital 6 days a week for many years.

48. He fought heavyweights and slugged toe-to-toe with several heavier fighters.

49. He worked long hours and studied long hours while getting his PhD.

50. He blocked and tackled guys much heavier than him at football.

51. He was the only person in the subway the day the Armenians threatened to bomb it.

52. He kept up his strength and endurance except when too sick or too preoccupied.

53. He did 40 chest thump, arms cut away pushups every day during football season.

54. He copes with a tough disease.

55. He is one of few schizophrenics to make something of himself. He fought hard to become a paramedical doctor.

56. He worked while coping with anxiety.

57. He copes with the effects of extreme introversion and shyness.

58. He coped with the feeling that people could read his mind.

59. He coped with hallucinations from all five senses.

60. He coped with delusions.

61. He coped with nasty voices with grace.

62. He coped with severe, intractable anger with grace.

63. He loved women.

64. He triumphed over sexual orientation concerns.

65. He took the bold step of marriage and cares for his wife, whom he loves dearly.

66. He coped with inferiority feelings with grace.

67. He overcame depression several times.

68. He coped with physical injury with grace.

69. He coped with rejection with grace.

70. He kept his faith in people

71. He drove himself to the point of pain and exhaustion sometimes while exercising.

72. He exercised while working full time.

73. He did 2-3 hours exercise for several months while working full time.

74. He socialized sometimes.

75. He coped with androphobia with grace.

76. He kept his cool most of the time when legitimately provoked to anger.

77. He exercised in bad weather.

78. He wrote in spite of the handicap of schizophrenia.

79. He coped with his girlfriend's and wife's problems with empathy.

80. He can see the good in people and forgive and forget.

81. He gave up his own interests in favor of the interests of others when he felt it necessary.

82. He excelled at academics learning to heal people in spite of a fragile schizophrenia that he did not know about.

83. He exercised through illness.

84. He excelled at manual labour, studying, and sports in spite of not being specifically suited to these.

85. He learned to cope with the anger and depression of his disease without resorting to suicidal behaviour. He is using these skills to help others.

86. He used the exercise high to decrease psychosis, anxiety, and depression and uses his experiences to help others.

87. He worked in nursing despite homophobia.

88. He coped with loneliness.

89. He coped with a strong sex drive while still maintaining morality.

90. He honoured his father and his mother after getting treatment for his disease.

91. He overcame a smoking phobia.

92. He started back disciplined activities after getting out of the habit.

93. He took canes away from a man who hit people and caused concussions.

94. He trained to overcome fear, danger, and pain with sports and relaxation training.

95. He went skydiving (dangerous-do not do).

96. Several women keep him sharp with powerful bareknuckle boxing. He does not hit women.

97. He stopped a man from being attacked and pushed onto the subway tracks and got attacked himself. He did not hit anyone.

98. He stopped to help a sick and homeless man and got abused by police for it.

99. He stops to help people who are poor, sick, and downtrodden.

100. He makes sure the needs of others are looked after before his own.

101. He keeps relatively fit in spite of depression and the negative symptoms of schizophrenia and several physical problems.

102. He kicked two men out of a store who were harrassing the owner. He did not hit them, but stood right in front of them and intimidated them with his fearlessness.

103. He did physical work in spite of painful tendonitis, arthritis, and degenerative disc disease.

104. He faced poverty and malnutrition and put his wife first to the extent she would allow.

105. He cleaned high rise windows unstrapped into a bosun's chair and risked plunging to his death.

106. Confidence in his ability to take a punch enabled him to stand up to several bullies.

107. He made educational history by being one of few people with a failing record in high school to be accepted into medical school and is one of few schizophrenics to achieve this.

108. He graduated from the college of hard knocks with honours.

109. And much, much more...

Printed in the United States
By Bookmasters